ASSEMBLY FOR CHRIST

ASSEMBLY
FOR
CHRIST

From Biblical Theology to
Pastoral Theology in the Twentieth Century

Thierry Maertens

DARTON, LONGMAN & TODD
London

First published in Great Britain in 1970 by
Darton, Longman & Todd Limited
85 Gloucester Road, London SW7
This translation © 1970 Darton, Longman & Todd Ltd,
Originally published in French by
Publications de Saint-André
© 1964 BIBLICA s.a., Quai au Bois Bruges, Belgium
Imprimi potest:
Abbatia Sti Andreae, die 19 Maii 1964.
+ Theodore Ghesquière, abbas.
Imprimatur:
Brugis, die 20 Maii 1964. + Mgr. De Keyzer, vic. gen.

Printed in Great Britain by
Western Printing Services Ltd Bristol

SBN 232 51069 5

CONTENTS

I

The contribution of the Old Testament

THE DESERT ASSEMBLY

EARLY MEANINGS OF 'QAHAL'

IN THE BEGINNING, the Hebrew *qahal* (sometimes translated into Greek by the word *synagōgē* or *ekklesia*) and its verb *qabaš* meant any kind of meeting. But from the earliest times these words acquired a precise, specialised meaning: for example, it became customary to speak of 'gathering', 'mustering' an army (Judg 12:4; Josh 9:2; 10:6; 1 Sam 28:1–4; 29:1; etc.), and because this word described the mobilisation of military forces to carry out the plans of a warrior God, not surprisingly it came to have religious implications (Ezek 38:4–15; 26:7; 23:24; 1 Kings 12:21; 1 Mac 3:13; Neh 4:14).[1]

We find the words *qahal* and *qabaš* used more often to describe a meeting of elders responsible for making official decisions (1 Sam 8:4; Judg 9:47). Greek texts often give this type of meeting the name *ekklesia* (Judg 6:16; 6:21; Deut 31:28), and this stresses its official role. This assembly, which represents the whole people, is entitled to make all the necessary decisions. The line is not sharply drawn between this gathering of notables or elders and that of the people themselves, as can be seen from a text like the following:

> They called together all the elders of the city, and their young men and their women ran to the assembly; and they set Achior with the people surrounding him, and Uzziah asked him what had happened (Jdt 6:16).

[1] For more elaborate semantic details, see Kittel and Tena-Barriga, *La palabra ekklesia estudio historico-teologico*, Barcelona 1958.

3

In any case, at this time the Jewish assembly of elders did not differ essentially from the meetings which regulated civic affairs in most Eastern countries. We need only recall its public character. It was summoned on the initiative of those in authority and membership was determined by the position a man held in the city.

These primitive meanings of the word *qahal* should not allow us to lose sight of its most obvious and widespread meaning (it occurs 160 times in the Old Testament), namely, the assembly of all the tribes. This chapter will concentrate on this more widespread meaning of the word and will seek to establish the exact period in which *qahal* took on this meaning and will attempt to discover the doctrinal process which made this possible. An inquiry of this kind can be successful, despite the occasional difficulties in dating biblical documents.

ANALYSIS OF DOUBLETS

To establish the origin of the doctrine of the assembly, we shall begin with an analysis of the doublets that are to be found in the last section of the first book of Samuel. The account of the death of Samuel comes to us in two distinct versions, one derived from ancient tradition, the other based on a more recent reading. In the older version, the king's death is soberly described:

> Now Samuel had died, and all Israel had mourned him, and they buried him in Ramah . . . (1 Sam 28:3),

while the more recent version introduces a new word:

> Now Samuel died; and all Israel *assembled* and mourned for him, and they buried him in his house at Ramah (1 Sam 25:1).

The same is true of the two versions which describe the bringing of the ark of the covenant to Jerusalem. In the eighth-century (?) narrative, David 'assembles' his troops to escort the ark (in the sense indicated above, 'to muster an army'):

> David again gathered all the chosen men of Israel, thirty thousand (2 Sam 6:1).

Yet in the third-century version this simple mustering of the soldiers becomes the summoning of the liturgical assembly of the whole people:

> David consulted with the commanders of thousands and of hundreds, with every leader. And David said to all the assembly of Israel, 'If it seems good to you, and if it is the will of the Lord our God, let us send abroad to our brothers who remain in all the land of Israel, and with them to the priests and Levites in the cities that have pasture lands, that they may come together to us. Then let us bring again the ark of our God to us; for we neglected it in the days of Saul.' All the assembly agreed to do so, for the thing was right[1] in the eyes of all the people.
>
> So David assembled all Israel from the Shinhor of Egypt to the entrance of Hamath, to bring the ark of God from Kiriath-jearim (1 Chron 13:1–5).

The descriptions of the reign of Asa given in *1 Kings* 15:9–24 (seventh century) and *2 Chronicles* 14–15 (third century) throw some light on this matter. In the oldest account, the king's biography concludes with a simple sentence:

> And Asa did what was right in the eyes of the Lord, as David his father had done (1 Kings 15:11).

The text of Chronicles is more explicit. As well as introducing legislative reforms, King Asa also took the initiative and, as the result of prophecy, summoned a great assembly of the people:

> When Asa heard these words, the prophecy of Azariah the son of Oded, he took courage, and put away the abominable idols from all the land of Judah and Benjamin and from the cities which he had taken in the hill country of Ephraim, and he repaired the altar of the Lord that was in front of the vestibule of the house of the Lord. And he gathered all Judah and Benjamin, and those from Ephraim, Manasseh, and Simeon who were sojourning with them, for great numbers had deserted to him from Israel when they saw that the Lord his God was with him. They were gathered at Jerusalem in the third month of the fifteenth year of the reign of Asa (2 Chron 15:8–10).

Chronicles obviously understood the king's life in the light of

---

[1] This is probably an allusion to a communal response similar to our *Dignum et justum* to which we will allude later.

an idea of the assembly, the details of which are discussed below. Here it should be noted that this assembly is summoned by the king; that it owes its origin to a prophecy; that it assumes ecumenical tendency because not only Judeans but Israelites were summoned; and it is set in a reforming context. The other main features of the assembly are: sacrifice (2 Chron 15:11), profession of faith (2 Chron 15:12), excommunication (2 Chron 15:13), and communal responses (2 Chron 15:14).

There are also two versions of the murder of Athaliah. According to the older tradition, her assassination is simply the result of a political plot and the assembly is almost entirely composed of soldiers who carry out the murder (2 Kings 11:4). In *Chronicles* 23, however, the conspirators become a liturgical assembly of the whole people which is the beginning of a reform of morals and the occasion of an excommunication of the wicked.

The same editorial revision emerges from comparison of the two versions of the reign of Ezekiel.[1] The Chronicler's version (2 Chron 29–30, third century) repeats the details given in *2 Kings* about the reign of Ezekiel (2 Kings 18, seventh century), adding two passages which contain descriptions of the two assemblies summoned by the king; the first for the purpose of reform (2 Chron 29:23, 28, 31, 32), the second as a sign of universalism (2 Chron 30). The Chronicler cannot report the life of a great king without mentioning one or other of the characteristic assemblies of his reign. Later we will analyse the content and meaning of both assemblies, to show the essential characteristics of the Jewish *qahal*: its ecumenical significance, its connection with the continuous reform of the people, its liturgical elements, the importance of the convocation and the Word, the meaning of the profession of faith and of the convenant made there. But here and now it can be concluded that the theology of the assembly and the term itself must have appeared some time between the seventh century, the date of the most recent version of 2 Kings, and the third century, when *Chronicles* was written. We have now to examine the different doctrinal trends that stand out during this four-century interval to discover the context in which the theology of the assembly developed.

[1] Cf. 1 Kings 8:14–21 and 2 Chron 6–7.

PRIESTLY LEGISLATION

The most immediate sources from which the Chronicler could have derived his great interest in the assembly can be traced to the priestly writings: Numbers, Leviticus, and some interpretations of Exodus, the whole belonging, practically speaking, to the fifth century. For this reason it is curious that the Greek translation of these books uses *synagōgē* for *qahal*, while the translator of Chronicles uses *ekklesia*. When the Septuagint was being written, the two Greek terms must have been practically synonymous.

Chronicles describes an assembly which is already well organised and important. The priestly writings, on the contrary, place it in a context of complaints and crises of authority and of structure (Num 14; 16; 17; 22; Exod 16:1-3). It would seem that, in its early stages, the Jewish assembly faced the same difficulties that were later to challenge the newly established Christian assembly (cf. 1 Cor). Despite these difficulties, an initial doctrinal synthesis was achieved, centred on God's holiness whence the assembly would derive its own holiness, provided it avoided uncleanness and all contact with the profane (Lev 4:16; Num 19:20).

There is a stress in several priestly texts on faith, loyalty to the rules given to the assembly by God, and the conditions necessary for his participation. Here, as often elsewhere in Scripture,[1] this faith is placed in sharp contrast with 'murmuring' the way in which most human affairs are conducted:

> Now there was no water for the congregation and they assembled themselves together against Moses and against Aaron. And the people contended with Moses, and said, 'Would that we had died when our brethren died before the Lord! Why have you brought the assembly of the Lord into this wilderness, that we should die here, both we and our cattle?' (Num 20:2-4).

> Then all the congregation raised a loud cry; and the people wept that night. And all the people of Israel murmured against Moses and Aaron; the whole congregation said to them, 'Would that we had died in the land of Egypt! Or would that we had died in this wilderness! Why does the Lord bring us into this land, to fall by

[1] See Exod 15:24; Jn 6:41, 46.

the sword? Our wives and our little ones will become a prey; would it not be better for us to go back to Egypt?' And they said to one another, 'Let us choose a captain, and go back to Egypt.' Then Moses and Aaron fell on their faces before the assembly of the congregation of the people of Israel (Num 14:1–5).

The problem is obvious. Either the assembly of Israel wants to imitate the assemblies of other nations and control its own policies, criticising decisions reached by its leaders; or it entrusts itself to the guidance of God and his representatives, Moses and Aaron, never losing sight of the fact that it is called together by God, and marks a necessary stage in the realisation of his plan for man.

During the fifth century, when these narratives were composed, several institutions were introduced that were designed to protect the life of the people after the exile. The throne of David was empty and the chair of Moses unoccupied, so the priests took it upon themselves to summon the people. Obviously, this development encountered difficulties. Comparing the opposition offered them to the murmurings and lack of faith in the first assembly, the priests called upon the people to acknowledge their rights to organise the assembly. The account of Korah's revolt is instructive. Korah and his associates represented the anti-sacerdotal groups:

and they assembled themselves against Moses and against Aaron, and said to them, 'You have gone too far! For all the congregation are holy, every one of them, and the Lord is among them;[1] why then do you exalt yourselves above the assembly of the Lord?' (Num 16:3).

The answer attributed to Moses shows what was in the minds of the fifth-century priestly writers:

is it too small a thing for you that the God of Israel has separated you from the congregation of Israel, to bring you near to himself, do service in the tabernacle of the Lord, and to stand before the congregation to minister to them; and that he has brought you near him, and all your brethren the sons of Levī with you? And would you seek the priesthood also? Therefore it is against the Lord that you and all

---

[1] This argument is based on Exod 19:6; 23:14. We will recognise this in the theology of the Old Testament which always tends to relapse into clericalism or democracy.

your company have gathered together; what is Aaron that you murmur against him? (Num 16:9–11).

Accounts like these reveal that the priests exercised an increasing ascendancy over the assembly, and they highlight for us its divine origin. In addition to the controversies they describe, an important meaning emerges from these passages. The assembly summoned by God does not depend on any human criteria. It cannot be reduced to these categories and anyone who would try to understand it from only this point of view can only 'murmur'. Thus, it is very important to realise that without faith the assembly remains on the level of simple human assemblies, even if they were assemblies for worship.

Lastly, the priestly texts show that the assembly was the ideal place for the sanctification of the people of God, that is, those who were separated from the human and profane world. This is strange because, while the purpose of the priestly assembly is to 'gather together', at the same time its function is to 'separate' by making holy. Entering the *qahal* is not the same thing as entering any other kind of group. Those who wish to take part must observe many purifying and expiating regulations that will set them apart from the world (Lev 16; 4:13–21), and excommunications preserve the assembly from the entrance of the unworthy:

> and the clean person shall sprinkle upon the unclean on the third day and on the seventh day; thus on the seventh day he shall cleanse him, and he shall wash his clothes and bathe himself in water, and at evening he shall be clean. But the man who is unclean and does not cleanse himself, that person shall be cut off from the midst of the assembly, since he has defiled the sanctuary of the Lord; because the water for impurity has not been thrown upon him, he is unclean (Num 19:19–20).

Later legislation, especially that which Judaism laid down, multiplied endlessly the regulations controlling admission to the assembly, and the numbers of those who were excluded increased: the lame and the blind (2 Sam 5:8; Lev 21:18), the pagans and 'the natives of the land' (Neh 10:31), and many more.

According to the priestly documents, the distinctive characteristic of the assembly is, therefore, the impossibility of reducing it to any human category. The assembly originated in God himself and was the place where God communicated his holiness; this was the reality which the assembly of the fifth century tried to express. This attempt led to a distinct crisis with obvious consequences. The priestly primacy was too exclusive and increasingly rigorous laws of purification and separation under-mined the existence of the assembly. But its supra-human character was nonetheless rigorously maintained. No sociology, no phenomenology, no 'history of religions' will ever be able to understand what it achieved. The assembly not only succeeded in uniting those who had 'gathered together' but perhaps even more those who were 'separated'. The summoning of all resulted in the sanctification of some. Its theoretical inclusive character was corrected by an actual exclusiveness.

To sum up what has already been said. In the beginning of this chapter, the comparison of doublets made it possible to assert that the doctrine of *qahal* appeared somewhere between the seventh and the third century. The study of the priestly docu-ments brought us to the fifth century where the doctrine of the assembly was examined, developed and questioned. By going back a century or two we come to the beginning of the theology of assembly.

DEUTERONOMIC LEGISLATION

Discovered in 622 in the temple of Jersualem, the statutes of Deuteronomy were proclaimed in the tribal assembly (2 Kings 23). Reform and spiritual progress were soon felt by the whole nation. The prophet Jeremiah spoke on behalf of the new legislation, while anonymous writers began to revise the old traditions of Genesis, Exodus and the other historical books in order to bring them into harmony with the new laws. This section is devoted to an examination of the statutes of Deuteronomy and all the texts which they influenced. It is worth mentioning here that the Greek translators of the Old Testament usually translated the *qahal* of the Deuteronomic texts by *ekklesia*, while the trans-lators of the priestly documents preferred the word *synagōgē*.[1]

[1] There are, however, some exceptions: Deut 10:4; Josh 18:1; 22:12; and Jeremiah.

The Deuteronomic revisers of Exodus made the gathering of
the Hebrew tribes around Sinai into a true assembly. Older
traditions (Exod 19–24) had attached little importance to this,
but as a result of the Deuteronomic reforms, the day when God
manifested himself to the people is repeatedly called the 'Day of
the Assembly' (Deut 4:10; 9:10; 10:4; 18:16):

> how on the day you stood before the Lord your God at Hōreb, the
> Lord said to me, 'Gather the people to me, that I may let them
> hear my words, so that they may learn to fear me all the days that they
> live upon the earth, and that they may teach their children so'
> (Deut 4:10).

The Hōreb assembly is centred not on sacrifices, as it will be
later under priestly influences, but on the Word of God as it is
expressed in the Decalogue:

> And the Lord gave me the two tables of stone written with the
> finger of God; and on them were all the words which the Lord had
> spoken with you on the mountain out of the midst of the fire on the
> day of the assembly (Deut 9:10).

The Word constitutes the assembly and the bearer of the Word,
whether legislator or prophet, automatically becomes its president:

> The Lord your God will raise up for you a prophet like me among
> you, from your brethren – him you shall heed – just as you desired
> of the Lord your God at Hōreb on the day of the assembly when you
> said, 'Let me not hear again the voice of the Lord my God, or see
> this great fire any more, lest I die' (Deut 18:15–16).

The assembly, therefore, owes its existence to the Word of
God. It is the Word that summons the assembly (Deut 4:10). It
is the Word that is read in the assembly (Deut 9:10). It is the
Word of the profession of faith that affirms membership (Deut
27:14–26).[1] And it is in the Word of a song of Moses that this
profession of faith is given expression:

> 'Assemble to me all the elders of your tribes, and your officers, that
> I may speak these words in their ears and call heaven and earth to

[1] This membership is expressed by *Amen* in Deuteronomy and in Neh 5:8–13.

witness against them . . .' Then Moses spoke the words of this song
until they were finished, in the ears of all the assembly of Israel . . .
(Deut 31:28, 30).

Before his death Moses laid down that an assembly similar to
the one in Hōreb should be held every seven years in Jerusalem
so that all might hear the Word and make a profession of faith:

> And Moses commanded them, 'At the end of every seven years, at
> the set time of the year of release, at the feast of booths, when all
> Israel comes to appear before the Lord your God at the place which
> he will choose, you shall read this law before all Israel in their hearing.
> Assemble the people, men, women, and little ones, and the sojourner
> within your towns, that they may hear and learn to fear the Lord
> your God, and be careful to do all the words of this law . . .'
> (Deut 31:10–12).

We know about some of these assemblies held in accordance
with what Moses prescribed. The writers of the Deuteronomic
elements of the Book of Joshua tried to show that the assembly of
Mount Ebal conformed to this law:

> And afterwards he read all the words of the law, the blessing and
> the curse, according to all that is written in the book of the law.
> There was not a word of all that Moses commanded which Joshua
> did not read before all the assembly of Israel, and the women, and
> the little ones, and the sojourners who lived among them (Josh
> 8:34–35).

The assembly which Solomon summoned for the dedication
of the temple also is Deuteronomic in inspiration. Although
explicit mention is not made of the reading of the Word, this
must have formed an essential element because the assembly was
summoned 'to honour Yahweh who had fulfilled his Word'
(1 Kings 8:20), and the word of Solomon praying to Yahweh in
the name of the people is the central act of the celebration (1
Kings 8:21–61).

More obviously 'Deuteronomic' is the assembly summoned by
Josiah precisely for the purpose of proclaiming the new law (2
Kings 23). Here we have the convocation (v.1), the reading of
the Word (v.2), the profession of faith and the making of the
covenant (v.3):

Then the king sent, and all the elders of Judah and Jerusalem were gathered to him. And the king went up to the house of the Lord, and with him all the men of Judah and all the inhabitants of Jerusalem, and the priests and the prophets, all the people, both small and the great; and he read in their hearing all the words of the book of the covenant which had been found in the house of the Lord. And the king stood by the pillar and made a covenant before the Lord, to walk after the Lord and to keep his commandments and his testimonies and his statutes, with all his heart and all his soul, to perform the words of this covenant that were written in this book; and all the people joined in the covenant (2 Kings 23:1-3).

The Deuteronomic movement, therefore, coincides with the origin of the assembly. It taught that the assembly was a divine convocation to hear God's Word and seal the covenant with him in a profession of faith. It also was aware that these elements which had recently appeared were only an expression of the potential contained in Hōreb assembly. Thus, the assembly marked a historic step in the accomplishment of God's plan announced on Sinai; more than a gathering for worship similar to pagan liturgical assemblies, it is a divine convocation centred around the Word of God and culminating in a covenant or a moral reform. Its ambition is to gather the people around the Word of God: almost all the texts insist on the fact that *all* the people should be present at the assembly, including women, children and even foreigners. Of course, the Deuteronomic assembly realised this universalism in a limited way by including in its number little more than the two tribes of Judah and Benjamin; but it was already aware of its fundamental ecumenical nature.

LATER ELEMENTS

Before gathering together all the information about the assembly given in the Old Testament, we must examine several ideas that, in the course of the history of Israel, were to enrich the doctrine of the assembly.

1. *The Expatriate Community.* Sent into exile, the people no longer have a homeland, they dwell among strangers (*paroikeō* Ps 120:6; 119:19), just like Abraham, 'the sojourner' (*paroikos*) *par*

excellence (Gen 21:34; 24:37; 26:2; 35:27). Naturally enough, therefore, when they returned to the Promised Land they were called 'the sons of Exile' (Ezra 8:35).

The biblical origins of the Community-in-exile ('parish') are still vague; the people were dimly aware of their nomad vocation, of their perpetual presence in a foreign land. The 'parish' theme developed independently of the assembly theme in biblical literature until Christians united them.

2. *The Assembly of the Separated Ones.* During the exile, the assembly was not summoned and Israel's national consciousness no longer had any expression. But as soon as the people began to enjoy conditions of relative freedom their leaders felt impelled to summon a new assembly (Neh 8–9) and this marks the historical date of renewal. Most of the elements of this restored assembly are familiar to us; they are the fruit of the different doctrinal movements which have structured and shaped the assembly since the days of Deuteronomy. National sentiments heightened by exile were expressed in a violent way. Laws of excommunication in priestly documents were rigorously enforced: all pagans and anyone connected with pagans were violently excluded from the assembly (Lam 1:10; Neh 13:1):

> And a proclamation was made throughout Judah and Jerusalem to all the returned exiles that they should assemble at Jerusalem, and that if any one did not come within three days, by order of the officials and the elders all his property shall be forfeited, and he himself banned from the congregation of the exiles. Then all the men of Judah and Benjamin assembled at Jerusalem within the three days . . . And Ezra the priest stood up and said to them, 'You have trespassed and married foreign women, and so increased the guilt of Israel. Now then make confession to the Lord the God of your fathers, and do his will; separate yourselves from the people of the land and from the foreign wives.' Then all the assembly answered with a loud voice, 'It is so; we must do as you have said . . .' (Ezra 10:6–12).

The two most characteristic features of this text are the exclusion of all foreigners from and the obligation of participation in the assembly. The sanction imposed in cases of the violation of these rules brings us close to the ghetto-assembly mentality of the next century:

> By these the king allowed the Jews who were in every city to gather and defend their lives, to destroy, to slay, and to annihilate any armed force of any people or province that might attack them, with their children and women, and to plunder their goods . . . (Esther 8:11). (Cf. Esther 9:2; 15–18.)

Without going to these extremes, however, the post-exilic assembly endeavoured to keep the nation free from all contacts with uncleanness. It not only summoned and gathered together, it also distinguished and separated. Judaism was to abuse these distinctions and these separations, but it is undeniable that even with these nationalist abuses, the assembly clearly expressed the conviction that it possessed the right to accept or refuse whatever it considered necessary. Fully aware of its mission and significance of this mission, the assembly recognised as its members those who were capable of carrying out the same mission and of expressing the same meaning.

3. *The Instruction Assembly.* Still another concept was added to the theology of the post-exilic assembly: 'the instruction assembly' which owed its origin to the widespread establishment of synagogues where the people were taught to 'assemble' around the wise men, the new presidents of the assembly (Sir 33:19). There the wisdom of the scribe was acclaimed:

> Nations will declare his wisdom,
> and congregations will proclaim
> his praise . . . (Sir 39:10).

> Peoples will declare their wisdom,
> and the congregation proclaims
> their praise . . . (Sir 44:15).

His charismatic gift was held in higher esteem than any other and his position was regarded as superior to that of manual workers (Sir 38:24–34).

This new type of assembly, the synagogue, claimed to possess the 'wisdom of God' and to be able to establish standards for moral life; it also believed that it enjoyed on the local level the functions of the national assembly. This is why it claimed to be the image of the assembly which the Most High holds in heaven:

> Wisdom will praise herself,
>   and will glory in the midst
>   of her people.
> In the assembly of the Most High
>   she will open her mouth,
> and in the presence of his host she will glory (Sir 24:1–2).

Inexact as this idea may be, the local assembly clearly assumes that, to a certain extent, God will be present.

The synagogal assembly is a repetition, as it were, of the Sinai assembly. The law which established the first was also read in the second; and the synagogal assembly considered itself responsible for the observance of this law and for the imposition of sanctions for its non-observance: the unfaithful wife

> will be brought before
>   the assembly,
> and punishment will fall on her children (Sir 23:24).

Because the assembly possesses the spirit of the covenant and the sign of its observance, this does not mean that it is indifferent to the life which goes on outside; it was believed that there should be unity and balance between the covenant proclaimed in the assembly and the covenant lived in daily life. Judaism discovered a new significance which the New Testament was to make more effective.

More important is the third characteristic of the synagogal assembly. In the writings of the last centuries, the term *qahal*, previously reserved for the great national assemblies of Jerusalem, was now applied to the smaller assemblies. Their purpose was merely instruction (Prov 5:14) or praise (Ps 22:23–26; 35:18; 40:10–11; 26:12), so that the Jew who took part in the local assembly was aware of the universalist and ecumenical purpose of the great national assembly, since what was contained in the universal and national *ekklesia* was experienced at the level of the particular *ekklesia*. The problem of the relations between the two assemblies was stated in Judaism and became the cornerstone of Christian theology concerning the assembly.

The Wisdom books brought little that was new to the doctrine of the assembly. However, there was a new awareness of God's presence in the assembly and an understanding of a relation between the local and the universal assembly; and this awareness, this development, was of major importance. It provides a groundwork on which Christians could base their thinking, and shows that the first Christians structured their own assemblies in perfect continuity with Old Testament thinking.

CONCLUSION: THE ELEMENTS OF THE JEWISH ASSEMBLY

Down the centuries of the history of Israel, the idea of assembly became increasingly meaningful.

The Deuteronomic movement which can rightly claim to have provided the first theology of assembly insists on the importance of the Word during the deliberations of the assembly; it also stressed the universal nature of the summons and of participation in the assembly.

The priestly documents reflect a serious crisis in the concept of the Jewish assembly. Because the presidency passed from the king and the prophets to the priests, more emphasis was put on the supernatural character of the assembly, showing it to be totally unlike any other kind of human assembly. Nothing profane or impure could be allowed to enter a place where God communicated his holiness. So true is this that its universalist nature, so important in the Deuteronomic point of view, was made much more apparent, mainly because there was a strong sense of the necessity to protect their rights among the priests.

Later writings, especially Chronicles, were the products of a period which had become much calmer, and during this time the assembly acquired a certain balance. The assembly once again became a sign of a general gathering together and a place from which great reforms could be initiated in the people's lives. It was always centred on the Word, but it was unable to free itself from a certain exclusiveness which, as it grew, particularly in Judaism, in the end stifled all ecumenical possibilities.

Lastly, without making any profound changes, the Wisdom

writings introduced some new elements: the idea of a divine presence in the assembly; the knowledge that participation in the assembly implied a moral witness in the lives of the participants; lastly and most importantly, awareness that the local assembly, no matter how small, was heir to the national and universal assembly.

The most meaningful conclusion we can give to this analysis of the Jewish assembly is to enumerate the classic elements of a celebration:

a) In the first place, emphasis must be given to the summoning of the assembly; it existed from the beginning and forms the root of the word qahal and of the word ekklesia. There are references to it in many descriptions of the assembly (1 Kings 8 : 1–2; 2 Chron 30; 15 : 8–10; etc.). It is the king who takes the initiative, or in the days of Moses, the prophet, the bearer of the Word of the covenant. Sometimes it was a prophet who urged the king to act. Men did not come together because they belonged to the same social or cultural categories, or because they shared the same ideas or because they wished to worship in the same way. These criteria could also be found in profane assemblies or in other religions. In Israel, only God or his representative summoned men to the assembly.

To speak of God's invitation is to transcend sociological or human categories. The invitation was universal, at least in intention; and when it was controlled by a small group – as it was often the case in Jewish history – all kinds of excommunications, which acted as a deterrent, were multiplied thereby reducing the assembly to an élite.

Yet this desire to excommunicate was not wholly negative. The assembly, or the president who had summoned it, reserved for himself the right to accept or reject any man who presented himself. Although it is true that the invitation was addressed to all, it was not to be regarded as a merely sociological phenomenon; obviously everyone could not at the outset grasp its full meaning. It could be understood on a too human level, so that only the secular meaning was appreciated and no attention was paid to the fact that it was an invitation to move into the realm of faith. It follows that the invitation is the expression of a form of jurisdictional power by which the assembly acknowledged its own members according to the faith they expressed in response to the invitation addressed to them.

b) When the assembly had gathered together, the predominant element in its celebration was *the reading of the Word of God*.

This reading of the law appeared for the first time during the assembly of Josiah (2 Kings 23), but it had an illustrious precedent; the reading of the law by Moses on Sinai before all the tribes of Israel (Deut 31:10–12). In the great assemblies of Moses, Josiah, Ezekiel and Nehemiah, the whole law was proclaimed.[1]

In the local synagogal assemblies, a certain reading was assigned to each sabbath according to a yearly or a five-yearly cycle. Only the scribes and doctors of the law had the right, as had once the kings and the prophets, to read this law. Shortly before the birth of Christ, as a result of the pressure of pietistic movements a second reading was added. This was a passage from the prophets which was shorter than the first reading and could be selected and read by any layman (over thirty).

It was the Word that constituted the assembly. This was the Word of the Covenant through which God proposed his plan to the people to make them a holy people, a royal priesthood, just as in the Sinai assembly. This was the Word which expressed God's will that they should turn to him, just as in the assemblies of Josiah and Nehemiah. This was the Word of history which makes the assembly a decisive step in the history of salvation.

c) The *homily* that traditionally follows the reading of the Word is meant to achieve these results: the call to turn towards God, the renewal of the Covenant, and an awareness of the history of salvation. The assembly is composed of intelligent men who were to understand the Word that had been proclaimed. This is the way Solomon puts it:

> Now the Lord had fulfilled his promise which he made . . . (1 Kings 8:20).

[1] See, for example, the detailed description given in Neh 8–9. Here the law should be understood to include the books of the Pentateuch.

The remark by Esdras, about the assembly after the return, puts it even more clearly:

> Also Joshua . . . and the Levites, helped the people to understand the law, while the people remained in their places. And they read from the book, from the law of God clearly, and they gave the sense, so that the people understood the reading (Neh 8:7–8).

The assembly, therefore, gives its members an 'understanding' that is called 'wisdom' in the synagogal assembly, and 'faith' in the Christian assembly. This mode of knowledge fulfils the ecumenical purpose of the convocation: all men do not have the same degree of intelligence or reason but they can all share the same wisdom and the same faith. Every word proclaimed in the assembly should not only be understood but, above all, should *edify*. St Paul asked the Corinthian assembly, which was far too eager for incomprehensible words and mysterious language, to recall this (1 Cor 14).

d) The proclamation of the Word and its explanation in the homily resulted in the solidarity of the assembled people. Reading and homily culminate in the *profession of faith*.

This profession of faith was given several expressions. The oldest seems to have been the communal responses: *Amen* or *It is right* or *It is our duty* (Neh 5:7–13; Ezra 10:12; Deut 27:11–26). These communal responses became so much a part of the assembly liturgy that they are still used in the Christian celebration.

Besides the communal responses, there were the songs. Deuteronomic tradition attributes to Moses a song that was meant to be a profession of faith for each important assembly (Deut 33). It appears in the Christian assembly at Easter.[1]

Other formulas were used to express this profession of faith: vows, resolutions, etc. (2 Chron 30; 2 Kings 23:3; Neh 8–9). They usually took the form of some kind of renewal of the covenant pact:

> And they entered into a covenant to seek the Lord, the God of their

[1] The elements that most successfully resist change in the history of liturgy are precisely those that are sung by the people, the communal responses, the hymns, etc. These elements move from one liturgy to another and many go back to the primitive Church, and even, as in this case, to Judaism.

fathers, with all their heart, and with all their soul; and whoever would not seek the Lord, the God of Israel, should be put to death, whether young or old, man or woman. They took oath to the Lord with a loud voice, and with shouting, and with trumpets, and with horns. And all Judah rejoiced over the oath; for they had sworn with all their heart, and had sought him with their whole desire, and he was found by them, and the Lord gave them rest round about (2 Chron 15:12–15).

We almost certainly know the exact words of this pact. Deuteronomy gives us the essential:

And the Levites shall declare to all the men of Israel with a loud voice: 'Cursed be the man who makes a graven or molten image, an abomination to the Lord, a thing made by the hands of a craftsman, and sets it up in secret.' And all the people shall answer and say, 'Amen'. 'Cursed be he who dishonours his father or his mother.' And all the people shall say, 'Amen'. 'Cursed be he who removes his neighbour's landmark.' And all the people shall say, 'Amen'. Cursed be he who misleads a blind man on the road.' And all the people shall say, 'Amen'. 'Cursed be he who perverts the justice due to the sojourner, the fatherless, and the widow.' And all the people shall say, 'Amen'. 'Cursed be he who lies with his father's wife, because he has uncovered her who is his father's.' And all the people shall say, 'Amen'. 'Cursed be he who lies with any kind of beast.' And all the people shall say, 'Amen'. 'Cursed be he who lies with his sister, whether the daughter of his father or the daughter of his mother.' And all the people shall say, 'Amen'. 'Cursed be he who lies with his mother-in-law.' And all the people shall say, 'Amen'. 'Cursed be he who slays his neighbour in secret.' And all the people shall say, 'Amen'. 'Cursed be he who takes a bribe to slay an innocent person.' And all the people shall say, 'Amen'. 'Cursed be he who does not confirm the words of this law by doing them.' And all the people shall say, 'Amen' (Deut 27:14–26).

e) Among the most expressive forms of the assembly's profession of faith should be mentioned the *sacrificial rite*. At the time of the first desert assembly, Moses presided at the celebration of the sacrifice to seal in some sort the pact signed by Yahweh and his people (Exod 24:1–11); and Solomon, wishing to give its full religious meaning to the assembly of the dedication of the temple, followed the same rite (1 Kings 8:62–66).

Even more than a simple gesture of worship, sacrifice is the expression of the assembly's faith and its obedient response to God's Word; more than a bloody immolation, it is a spiritual sacrifice that derives its significance from the opening profession of faith. The descriptions of the assembly are more detailed concerning the people's profession of faith than about the sacrificial rite, and synagogal assemblies like that of Nehemiah could be perfectly planned and organised without any sacrificial rite. The latter, therefore, is not an absolutely necessary element or more exactly, it is important because it is the spiritual response that the assembly should make to God's Word.

Nothing like this is to be found in the assemblies of other religions which are centred on the offering of a sacrifice. In Israel the invitation, the proclamation of the Word and its interpretation, and finally the profession of faith give the sacrifice a unique significance that transcends the purely religious and worshipping character of pagan sacrifices and is, in fact, a sign of obedience and submission to God's will. At the same time, it is an act of thanksgiving which rises from man's heart when he recalls the wonders wrought by God for man's salvation.

f) In addition to, or instead of, the profession of faith or the sacrifice, mention is often made of *the prayer of the president*, the blessing or the thanksgiving. This element belongs to the same category as the other two, it signifies the assembly's response to the Word of God. The most detailed description of the president's prayer found in the Bible is that of Solomon in 1 Kings 8. The king addresses to God a prayer of thanksgiving before proceeding to the sacrificial rites and as if to give them their real meaning:

> Then Solomon stood before the altar of the Lord in the presence of all the assembly of Israel, and spread forth his hands toward heaven; and said, 'Oh Lord, God of Israel, there is no God like thee, in heaven above or on earth beneath . . . Now therefore, O lord, God of Israel, keep with thy servant David my father what thou hast promised him . . . Now therefore, O God of Israel, let thy word be confirmed, which thou has spoken . . . hearken thou to the supplication of thy servant and of thy people Israel, when they pray towards this place . . . If a man sins against his neighbour . . . When thy people Israel are defeated before the enemy . . . When heaven

is shut up and there is no rain . . . If there is famine in the land . . .'
(Solomon) stood and blessed all the assembly of Israel with a loud
voice, saying, 'Blessed be the Lord who has given rest to his people
Israel . . .' (1 Kings 22–60).

In this prayer it seems possible to discover the four elements
that are characteristic of every eucharistic prayer included in
Christian assemblies: the thanksgiving to the God of Israel who is
paramount in heaven and earth, the anamnesis ('memorial') of his
plan ('the promise that you have made'), the epiclesis which, in
the form of a litany, lists the needs of the people so that God may
answer them, and the final doxology.

g) The celebration of the assembly is thereby completed: man's
word has replied to God's Word; thanksgiving has expressed
man's understanding of God's plan as it was newly revealed in the
proclamation of the Word; the profession of faith has sealed the
promise which was made in response to the demands of the Word.
A final element closed the assembly: *the dismissal*. This element
held an important place in the Jewish doctrine of the assembly.
Proof of this can be found in the imposing number of accounts of
assemblies which contain allusions to it: 1 Kings 8:66; Jos
24:28; 2 Chron 7:10; 2 Chron 31:1.

On the twenty-third day of the seventh month he sent the people
away to their homes, joyful and glad of heart for the goodness that the
Lord had shown to David and to Solomon and to Israel his people
(2 Chron 7:10).

The function of the dismissal corresponds to that of the
invitation. Each is reserved to the president of the assembly in
order to keep intact its official character. Each marks the
frontiers of the assembly in relation to daily life and distinguishes
the people-event from the institution-event. The assembly is, in
fact, the event that has just given meaning to man's institutions
and attitudes. It is a stage in a life which is still basically nomadic.

The assembly is composed of, and represents the people, but
this does not convey the whole meaning. The invitation is a form
of recognition of the pre-eminence of the assembly over all the
other functions of the people, but the dismissal is an acknow-
ledgment that the assembly is not the whole people. Thus the

dismissal establishes a relation between the assembly and daily life. It establishes a continuity between the work of the assembly inspired by the Word of God, and the work of daily life based on fidelity to the pact sealed in the assembly, in obedience to the Word proclaimed and ratified. Israel had a profound experience of this continuity. If the assemblies of Josiah, Asa, and Ezekiel were able to initiate reform, it was because they believed that they possessed the power to judge and evaluate the conduct of their members and were able to exclude those who failed to live up to the obligations they had contracted in the assembly. Later centuries saw the deepening of this relation between the assembly and the dismissal to ordinary life, between the assembly-event and the institutions of the people. They looked forward to an assembly in which there would be no dismissal, the eternal assembly in which the acts of witnessing and celebrating would be fused, in which the event and the institution would coincide in one and the same reality.

Thus, as early as the Deuteronomic reform, the essential elements of the assembly were already united, solidly structured and balanced, their purpose clearly understood. We are still only at the beginning of the history of the assembly, yet throughout its whole development, passing from Judaism to Christianity, this structure was preserved and strengthened because new doctrinal progress cast new lights and revealed new needs while always respecting the original content.

THE ASSEMBLY OF THE RETURN

After the dispersion and the return to the Promised Land, the Jewish assembly, which before the Exile had remained similar to the desert assembly and the renewal of the Sinai covenant, acquired a new character.

While the priests, who had become largely responsible for the Jewish assembly and who were gradually changing its meaning, now placed excessive emphasis on its separation from the world and included larger numbers of men in its interdicts, the prophets remained faithful to the primitive concept of the assembly, especially to its ecumenical character and the divine initiative in man's call to salvation. To them, the return from exile and consolidation of the dispersed Jews was a form of a divine call to the liturgical assembly. Thus God became the great 'Assembler' of his people, transforming his call into a pardon and a (moral) resurrection to ensure the success of the future assembly.

It was along these lines that the Deuteronomist and the prophet Jeremiah described the consolidation of the scattered Jews:[1]

'I will be found by you,' says the Lord, 'and I will restore your fortunes and gather you from all the nations and all the places where I have driven you,' says the Lord, 'and I will bring you back to the place from which I sent you into exile' (Jer 29:14).

Jeremiah also believed that this assembly was entrusted to the 'shepherd of the flock':

Then I will father the remnant of my flock out of all the countries where I have driven them, and I will bring them back to their fold, and they shall be fruitful and multiply (Jer 23:3; cf. 31:7–10; 32:37).

Micah (2:12; 4:6) seems to have been the first prophet to unite the themes of assembly, shepherd and Zion, the centre of the future assembly, but it was Ezekiel who understood this better than anyone else. At the beginning of his ministry, he confined himself to repeating the principal prophecies of Jeremiah on the subject of the assembly:

Therefore say, 'Thus says the Lord God: "I will gather you from the peoples, and assemble you out of the countries where you have been scattered, and I will give you the land of Israel" ' (Ezek 11:17; cf. 28:25).

He also followed Jeremiah in the use of the image of the 'shepherd who calls an assembly':

And I will bring them out from the peoples, and gather them from the countries, and will bring them into their own land; and I will feed them with good pasture, and upon the mountain heights of Israel by the fountains, and in all the inhabited places of the country (Ezek 34:13).

[1] The Deuteronomist believed that Jerusalem was the only valid place for assembly (Deut 12:2–12).

While this doctrinal synthesis was being developed, Ezekiel offered new details about the eschatological assembly. Certainly one of the most interesting of these was the relation that he established between the future assembly and the old desert assembly, the events that were a prelude to the latter would be renewed by a similar preparation for the former:

'I will bring you out from the peoples and gather you out of the countries where you are scattered, *with a mighty hand and an out-stretched arm*, and with wrath poured out; and *I will bring you into the wilderness* of peoples, and *there I will enter into judgment* with you face to face. *As I entered into judgment with your fathers in the wilderness of the land of Egypt*, so will I enter into judgment with you,' says the Lord God. 'I will make you pass under the rod, and I will let you go in by number. *I will purge out the rebels* from among you, and *those who trangress against me*; *I will bring them out of* the land where they sojourn, *but they shall not enter the land of Israel*. Then you will know I am the Lord.' . . . 'As a pleasing odour I will accept you, when I bring you out from the peoples, and gather you out from the countries where you have been scattered; and *I will manifest my holiness* among you in the sight of nations' (Ezek 20:34–38, 41).

The most important phrases of this passage have been italicised above. They are all borrowed from accounts of the Exodus and the sojourn in the desert. Thus, the desert assembly is not only a past event that later assemblies attempt to reproduce, and to which they intend to remain faithful (this is the position of the Deuteronomist); it also becomes the model of the future assembly which will gather together for the first time all those who have returned from exile and will signify the country's recovered national unity and political rebirth.

This point of view is essential to the later evolution of Jewish assemblies. Before the exile when they gathered together in assembly, the Jews looked back to the past and recalled the desert assembly in which the covenant had been made. Henceforth all their assemblies were to be based on the hope and expectation of the great assembly which was to re-fashion the Chosen People and during which a new covenant would be made, eclipsing the first:

'For I will take you from the nations, and gather from all the countries, and bring you into your own land. I will sprinkle clean water upon you, and you shall be clean from all your uncleanness, and from all your idols I will cleanse you' (Ezek 36:24–25; cf. 39:27).

In these words the prophet Ezekiel finds an eschatological meaning in the assembly. To assemble today, although only locally and in a small group, is in some ways even now to prepare for and to live the eschatological assembly which God will call when his plan is fulfilled. This will be the sign the people have been restored and the complete realisation of the ecumenical project which belongs to each assembly.

There is no mistaking the fact that the God of Israel is God the Assembler *par excellence*, and that his plan of salvation for men consists in drawing all men to him. He began to do this on Sinai and will not cease until men – or at least Israel – are integrated in the permanent assembly:

> Thus says the Lord God,
>   who gathers the outcasts of Israel,
> I will gather yet others to him
>   besides those already gathered (Isa. 56:8).

One of the first benefits of the new assembly will be to manifest its universal character by the reunion of all the tribes of Israel previously separated by the schism:

' . . . I will take the people of Israel from the nations among which they have gone and will gather them from all sides, and bring them to their own land; and I will make them one nation in the land, upon the mountains of Israel; and one king will be king over them all; and they shall be no longer two nations, and no longer divided into two kingdoms' (Ezek 37:21–22).

When the Jews returned from exile, the idea of an assembly of both kingdoms seemed rather utopian. Few Hebrews were able to say to which tribe they belonged. But when Ezekiel decided to carry out Hezekiah's unfortunate project (2 Chron 30), he made it very clear that in the assemblies summoned by God, men came together without regard to human categories or any of the divisions and separations caused by nature, temperament, money or worldly factors.

This prophetic strain had deepened the doctrine of the assembly by giving it an eschatological purpose; namely, to prefigure God's great assembly and realise it by uniting men who are separated by all else except the divine plan.

THE ASSEMBLY OF THE NATIONS

Reflecting on the universal purpose of the assembly, increasingly the prophets came to understand that they should welcome other nations and not limit themselves to the Chosen People. If they were to exclude all other peoples would this not be an injustice to God-the-Assembler and restrict application of his plan of salvation to one people alone?

It cannot be denied that the Jews were slow to accept the idea of an international assembly. Did they not recall with sorrow the assembling of the nations at Jerusalem in order to destroy the city (Zeph 3:8; Ezek 16:37; 23:24; 39:17; Mic 4:11–12; Isa 34:15–16; Jer 49:14)?

The first prophets who thought of a future assembly of the nations in Jerusalem did so in terms of an assembly which met to judge and condemn the nations and to avenge Israel:

I will gather all the nations and bring them down to the valley of Jehoshaphat, and I will enter into judgment with them there, on account of my people and my heritage Israel, because they have scattered them among the nations and have divided up my land . . . (Joel 3:2; cf. 3:11).

Let all the nations gather together,
    and let the peoples assemble.
Who among them can declare this,
    and show us the former things?
Let them bring witnesses to justify them,
    and let them hear and say, It is true (Isa 43:9).

This notion corresponds fairly closely with the general view prevalent at Nehemiah's great assembly (8–9), where every effort was made to separate the Chosen People from all other men.

The third-Isaish declared with the same spirit of vengeance

that all the nations would one day submit to the future assembly
on Zion:

> And nations shall come to your light,
>   And kings to the brightness of your rising.
> Lift up your eyes round about, and see;
>   they all gather together, they come to you . . .
> All the flocks of Kedar shall be gathered to you . . .
> For the coastlands shall wait for me,
>   the ships of Tarshish first . . . (Isa 60:3–9).

Probably this vision should be interpreted in a restricted sense.
It may be wondered whether the author of this prophecy regards
the nations as truly called to take part in this assembly or as
merely charged with the return of the exiles to their own country,
thus performing an act of reparation for their persecution of the
Chosen People; their reunion with the Jewish people would be a
real sign of God's calling all men to union.

Not until the prophetic texts of the fifth and fourth centuries
do we find the announcement of an assembly that includes other
nations as well as Israel. In the final oracles of the third-Isaiah a
prophecy foretells that the nations will take part in the assembly
and will then exercise the priestly duties hitherto reserved for
the Chosen People. The assembly will even become missionary in
purpose and the participants will believe that they have been sent
to the peoples to call them to union with themselves:

'For I know their works and their thoughts, and I am coming to
gather all nations and tongues; and they shall come and shall see my
glory and I will set a sign among them. And from them I will send
survivors to the nations, to Tarshish, Put and Lud, who draw the
bow, to Tubal and Javan, to the coastlands afar off, that have not
heard my fame or seen my glory; and they shall declare my glory
among the nations. And they shall bring all your brethren from all
the nations as an offering to the Lord, upon horses and in chariots,
and in litters and upon mules, and upon dromedaries, to my holy
mountain Jerusalem, says the Lord, just as the Israelites bring their
cereal offering in a clean vessel to the house of the Lord. And some
of them also I will take for priests and for Levites,' says the Lord
(Isa 66:18–21).

There are undertones of 'revenge' in this oracle. There is an insistent demand that the nations must make reparation and bring the exiles back to Jerusalem. Its aim is still far too centri-petal: the universal assembly is localised in Zion. With this reservation, this oracle is one of the summits of Old Testament religious experience. The return of the exiles is an act of worship similar to that in which the children of Israel bring their offering to the altar.

The sacrifice offered in the temple will thenceforth be not only one of burnt-offering and communion but a spiritual sacrifice available to all men, an act of faith and obedience in accordance with the plan of assembly ordained by God. Zachariah confirms this. He prescribes a purified and simplified sacrificial ceremonial so that the nations may take part in the eschatological assembly in Jerusalem:

> Then every one that survives of all the nations that have come against Jerusalem shall go up year after year to worship the King, the Lord of hosts, and to keep the feast of booths. And if any of the families of the earth do not go up to Jerusalem to worship the King, the Lord of hosts, there will be no rain upon them . . . And on that day there shall be inscribed on the bells of the horses, 'Holy to the Lord'. And the pots in the house of the Lord shall be as the bowls before the altar; and every pot in Jerusalem and Judah shall be sacred to the Lord of hosts, so that all who sacrifice may come and take of them and boil the flesh of the sacrifice in them. And there shall no longer be a trader in the house of the Lord of hosts on that day (Zech 14:16–17; 20–21).

The prophet, therefore, goes much further than his predeces-sors. In Jerusalem he sees so great an assembly that the sacred vessels of the temple will not suffice and profane vessels will have to be brought from private kitchens so that all the sacrifices may be offered.[1] The merchants will leave the temple because all the offerings will have been accepted; there will no longer be any need for exchange or barter.[2]

The third-Isaiah goes further still. He foresees that the future

---

[1] This is a reminder of Solomon's assembly where the offerings were so numerous that the whole temple court had to be used as an altar so that all the sacrifices that had been presented could be offered.

[2] At least that seems to be our Lord's interpretation in Mt 21:12–17. Cf. infra p. 41.

assembly will be missionary and that its members will be sent by God to the nations and distant lands (Isa 66:19–20). What does this mean? At the very least it shows that Yahweh intends to attain his goal of assembling all nations by means of a 'sign' (verse 18) which is none other than the assembly itself. Participation in this assembly means the recognition that it marks an advance in the divine plan of the assembly and includes, as a logical consequence, taking part in the mission that effectively fulfils this plan.

The first Christians had a better understanding of the fact that the liturgical assembly is an act by which God has already gathered mankind together. They saw the close connection between the mission that seeks to bring about the assembly of all men in the Church and the mystery contained in the liturgical assembly.

We should not impute this theology to the third-Isaiah who did no more than discover its possible approaches, but it cannot be denied that the theology of the assembly owed much to the prophets, not so much because they added new elements but because they deepened existing ones. Because of the ecumenical nature of the assembly they were able to discover the assembly of the nations. Because of the divine summons, which is the origin of every assembly, they recognised God as the great 'Assembler'.

Thus, several aspects of the assembly gradually become clearer: the necessity of a spiritual sacrifice in which people of different cultures could be reunited; the missionary activity of the assembly which is the sign that it was God's assembly; the eschatological significance of every gathering of this kind which was an advance towards the great, definitive assembly that can already be anticipated; lastly, the unity between what is celebrated in the assembly and what takes place in daily life.[1]

The prophetic movement was probably halted by the Jewish priestly institutions which were more concerned about separation and excommunication than with convocations and assemblies; they were more interested in the 'pure' of the Jewish

[1] The best study of the liturgical assembly and the spiritualising effort of the prophets is by Gary, *Les prophètes et le culte à partir de l'exil*, Desclée, Tournai 1960.

élite than with all those who came from the different nations. But the teaching of the prophets was to be preserved by certain Jewish sects, and the first Christians, not without a certain hesitation, were able to integrate this teaching into the structures of the Church and the assembly.

THE SIGNIFICANCE OF THE ASSEMBLY IN THE OLD TESTAMENT

In order to interpret all the many facts that our investigation of the Old Testament has provided, we shall try to see how a Jew, strongly influenced by Scripture and deeply concerned about the meaning of his religious acts, took part in the local assembly, in the synagogue, or the national assembly in Jerusalem.

When the Jew gave the name *ekklesia* to these assemblies, he knew that he was using a profane word frequently found in Greek literature, a word which denoted the assembly of the people regularly summoned by competent authority, to which authorised heralds were sent to note and, when necessary, to ratify the decisions reached by those in office.

But, as we can see in the Books of Maccabees, the term *ekklesia*, in spite of its profane associations, did not prevent a Jew from noticing what distinguishes the gathering in which he took part from the political, pagan assemblies.

First of all, he realised that it was God himself and not just any political authority who summoned the assembly. In fact, the Jew regarded these political authorities – even his own – with a certain disdain because, instead of gathering together, they did nothing but disperse and separate (Jer 10:21; Ezek 34:5–6). He knew that God alone had the power to assemble and that the salvation he would one day give his people would be in the form of a vast assembly. Legend even asserted that the objects needed for this worship would remain hidden until the day of this future assembly (2 Mac 2:7).

God made his desire to save all men so clear that the Jews knew that the future assembly would include all nations. Yet he knew that they would be placed in a subordinate position as just punishment for the sufferings that they had inflicted on the Chosen

People. Yet this did not prevent the pagans from truly participating in the assembly and in the spiritual sacrifice which would be celebrated there. Thus assembly and mission became complementary notions, two aspects of one and the same design of God the Assembler.

If the faithful Jew had been asked to choose one word to define the eschatological assembly to which he was called, he would have used the word 'catholic' or 'universal'. He looked back with too much nostalgia to the old assemblies where all the tribes were united and he looked forward with too much hope to the future assemblies where all nations would meet, not to attach great importance to the idea of ecumenicity and to hope, perhaps, that his little local synagogue assembly could reflect this open and welcoming dimension.

Proof of this may be seen in the fact that he did not hesitate to give it the same name – *ekklesia* – that he gave to the great national assemblies and to the eschatological assemblies of the nations; he was already aware that his local assembly was at least the sign pointing to and preparing for the universal assembly.

Nevertheless, the local assembly to which the Jew was summoned contained within itself a contradiction that Judaism made even more acute. To this assembly the 'clean' alone were invited while a series of interdicts and excommunications were directed against all those who incurred legal or moral uncleanness, or who had contacts with the pagan world. This massive exclusion of those outside the assembly corresponded to an exaggerated specialisation of functions within. There was excessive clericalism, a most exact division of places of honour and a meticulous protocol. Because of these exclusions and rigidity of structure, the Jew could easily forget the catholicity of his assembly.

In this way the Jewish assembly, itself a sign of God's plan, tended to thwart the realisation of this plan, dividing what was meant to be united and separating what was meant to be assembled. Since the days of Moses, the prophets had been responsible for the assembly, its meaning and its structure. So a prophet was needed to recall these essential elements and to restore to the assembly its first mission of being the first step in God's great assembling of all mankind.

2

The work of the assembly of Christ

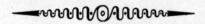

THIS CHAPTER CONTAINS an analysis of Christ's attitude to the Jewish assembly and a study of his intentions for the Christian assembly. The next chapter will be devoted to an examination of the relevant passages in the epistles and Acts. This division may sound easy but from an exegetical point of view it does not accurately correspond with the facts. Indeed, it is obvious that the writers of the Gospels recalled Christ's teaching about the assembly because they were addressing Christian assemblies then in quest of their own structure and meaning. The motives that led the evangelists to collect Christ's words about the assembly are the same that impelled St Paul to write to the Corinthians about the structure of their assembly and led St Luke unobtrusively to establish a parallel between the assembly of Jerusalem and Antioch in his book of Acts. Thus the division into two chapters, one dealing with the gospel texts and the other with the rest of the New Testament, is somewhat artificial. But I think that the reader will find this division helpful.

CHRIST THE ASSEMBLER

On several occasions the gospel tradition presents Christ as one who is charged with fulfilling the plan of assembly attributed to Yahweh by the Old Testament prophets:

O Jerusalem, Jerusalem, killing the prophets and stoning those who are sent to you! How often would I have gathered your children together as a hen gathers her brood under her wings, and you would not! Behold, your house is foresaken and desolate. For I tell you, you will not see me again, until you say, 'Blessed is he who comes in the name of the Lord' (Mt 23:37–39).

In St Matthew's gospel this passage effects the transition between the curses against the Scribes and Pharisees, which emphasise the failure of the old order, and the eschatological discourse which looks forward to the time of the new assembly after the fall of Jerusalem. The Messiah's intention is clear. He is just at the end of his public life and one after another different groups of the people have left him. On the eve of his passion, practically alone, he faces the apparent failure of his mission of assembling the people. Jerusalem and the Temple had refused to be the instruments through which he could work. And so Jerusalem had no longer any reason to exist. It would soon be caught up in the whirlpool of history and would shortly be wiped off the map (cf. Mt 24). The Temple where the nations were meant to gather would be left empty.

Obviously Christ's Jewish contemporaries would think such a prediction blasphemous. The destruction of Jerusalem and of the Temple implied that all the prophecies of the Old Testament foretelling a gathering together of the nations in this place were untrue and would lose their credibility; even the Word of God was called in question.

The evangelists collated other texts enabling the first Christians to understand that the old centres of assembly would be replaced by a new centre which would be none other than the risen Christ. This idea is expressed in the passage of Matthew 23 just quoted.

This idea that the Son of Man will take the place of the Temple can be found in the trial of Jesus:

> At last two came forward and said, 'This fellow said, "I am able to destroy the Temple of God and to build it in three days . . ." "I tell you, hereafter you will see the Son of man seated at the right hand of Power, and coming on the clouds of heaven" ' (Mt 26:61–65).

Christ did indeed foretell the destruction of the Temple, but he immediately substituted his own person for it, presenting himself as the Son of Man whom Daniel had foretold would preside over the meeting of the nations:

> And to him was given dominion
> and glory and kingdom,

> that all peoples, nations, and languages
>   should serve him;
> his dominion is an everlasting dominion,
>   which shall not pass away,
> and his kingdom one
>   that shall not be destroyed (Dan 7:14).

Notice that the Son of Man will come on the clouds – not at the end of time – but as soon as the Temple is destroyed (Mt 26:64). Another passage also inspired by Daniel 7:14 teaches the same lesson:

> Immediately after the tribulation of those days the sun will be darkened . . . then will appear the sign of the Son of man in heaven, and all the tribes of the earth will mourn, and they will see the Son of man coming on the clouds of heaven with power and great glory; and he will send out his angels with a loud trumpet call, and they will gather his elect from the four winds, from one end of the heaven to the other (Mt 24:29–31).[1]

A somewhat rigid exegesis regards this text as a description of the Last Judgment. Without denying this entirely, Christ means that the work of the assembly which, until the fall of Jerusalem, was entrusted to that city, now depends on the initiative of 'the Son of Man coming in the clouds', that is, the risen Christ in all his power and glory (cf. Mt 12:40),[2] and served by angels who are probably not the angels of heaven but 'those who are sent', the apostles and missionaries (Rev 2:1, 8, 12, 18; 3:1, 7, 14). Instead of the trumpets that called the Jews to worshipping assemblies (Lev 21:23–24; Ps 47:1–7), we have the trumpet of the Good News and the proclamation of the assembly of the nations.

A text in some ways parallel may be found in 2 Thess 2:1–8. The Thessalonians knew that the coming of the Lord would also mean the gathering together of all mankind with Christ. Paul

---

[1] Although he seems at times to force the argument, A. Feuillet gives an interesting exegesis of chapter 24 in *La synthèse eschatologiques de saint Matthieu*, Rev. Bibl. 1949 (pp. 340–364); 1950 (pp. 62–91); 1950 (pp. 180–211).
[2] It is curious to see that many New Testament texts contrast the temple with the Son of Man (Mt 24:30; 26:61–64; Jn 1:51; Acts 7:47–56). This suggests a tradition derived from Qumrân or from some special Jewish sect: A. Klijn, *Stephen's Speech*, N.T.S. 1957, pp. 25–31.

revealed to them the preparatory signs for this assembly and like Matthew 24, he recalls that the 'man of iniquity' must first appear in the Temple (2 Thess 2:4–5; cf. Mt 24:15). Once the Temple has been profaned and its mission of assembly has thus been made ridiculous, the true assembly can set to work and the Lord can 'come' (2 Thess 2:8; cf. Mt 24:30–31; 26:64) to establish his dominion over the world.

Later doctrinal speculation was to interpret this 'gathering' presence of the Lord and from it drew pastoral conclusions. These conclusions will be examined below. For the moment it will suffice for us to share the faith of these first Christians as they free themselves from the promises made about Jerusalem and find their true fulfilment in the person of him who is above powers and principalities (Col 1:15–20), and whose sovereign function consists in gathering all nations in himself. It is no longer a place but a living person who gathers together; and the assembly is possible only for those who share in the mysterious life of this person.

AN ASSEMBLY OPEN TO ALL

At the heart of the Jewish assembly there was a deep contradiction because its universalism was belied by its exclusive and separatist regulations. The primitive Christian community, as heir to this assembly, must have quickly questioned the validity of these regulations. Should it, because of its ecumenical vocation, set aside these various categories of the 'unclean'? Christians only gradually discovered the right answer to this question. In the next chapter we shall see that this was not always done smoothly and without some hesitation. But the gospels provided a solution. Whenever Christ spoke as an 'assembler', he summoned all the categories excluded from the Jewish assembly.

'The blind and the lame' were the first to benefit. A mysterious story which comes to us only in a very corrupt text sought to justify the exclusion of these men from the Jewish assembly:

The blind and the lame shall not come into the house (2 Sam 5:8).

On the other hand, whenever Christ had occasion to bring

them into the Temple assembly, he did not hesitate to cure them first so that they might enter.[1] This is why Christ first purified the Temple and expelled buyers and sellers, then summoned the lame and the blind:

And the blind and the lame came to him in the temple, and he healed them. But when the chief priests and the scribes saw the wonderful things that he did . . . they were indignant (Mt 21:14–15).

Luke, who was addressing a Greek public unacquainted with these Jewish prohibitions, does not relate this episode. Yet he is by no means indifferent to the extension of the invitation to the blind and lame, and he inserts this theme in his parable of the banquet which is another image of the Christian assembly:

So the servant came and reported this to his master. Then the house-holder in anger said to his servant, 'Go out quickly to the streets and lanes of the city and bring in the poor and maimed and blind and lame' (Lk 14:21).

He returns to the same theme in his description of Peter's first miracle, the cure of a lame man so that he could enter the Temple (Acts 3). This insistence of the evangelists to stress Christ's attitude to summoning the 'unclean' to the assembly was no doubt a response to the problems raised by the first Christians, especially by those who had come from Judaism and were inclined to transfer to the Christian assembly the prohibitions that pre-served the Jewish assembly from all contact with the sick.

The parable of the wedding banquet (Lk 14:16–24 and Mt 22:1–14) alluded to above, could be regarded as the charter of invitation to the Christian assembly (notice the words 'summon', 'send for', and 'invite', Mt 22:3, 4, 9).[2] Note that in the version found in Matthew, this summons could only be issued after the destruction of the 'city':

The king was angry and he sent his troops and destroyed those murderers and burned their city. Then he said to his servants, 'The

[1] The summons turns into a healing when necessary. It becomes absolution when those who are called are sinners. On p. 52, we shall see the connection between the sacrament of pardon and the assembly.

[2] See R. Swaeles, L'orientation 'ecclésiastique' de la parabole du festin nuptial en Mt. 22. Eph. Th. Lov. 1960, pp. 655–684.

wedding is ready but those invited were not worthy. Go therefore to the thoroughfares, and invite to the marriage feast as many as you find' (Mt 22:7–9).

Here we find the concept of 'Christ the Assembler' that had already been expressed in the many texts which took from Jerusalem and gave to the risen Lord the right to summon men to the assembly. In this parable the servants of the king perform the 'mission' entrusted to the angels in the eschatological discourse.[1] They represent the mission of the Church to the nations after the disappearance of Jerusalem, thus fulfilling the divine plan of summoning and of assembling.

St Luke specifies the categories of men who are summoned. They are the 'poor' and the 'pagans':

Go out quickly to the streets and lanes of the city and bring in the poor and maimed and blind, and lame. . . . Go out to the highways and hedges, and compel people to come in, that my house may be filled (Lk 14:21–23).[2]

Besides the 'unclean' of Israel, which included both the blind and lame, the Christian assembly also summons members of pagan nations. Other categories which Judaism more or less excluded from the assembly found themselves included in Christ's summons. Among them were sinners and publicans. St Matthew pointed out that the servants who went out to deliver invitations to the wedding

gathered all whom they found, both bad and good; so the wedding hall was filled with guests (Mt 22:10).

Assembling became a 'gathering together' and the assembly 'a crowded hall'. This wording makes clear the inclusion of 'everyone' and the willingness to scandalise the aesthetes who would have liked to keep the assembly 'clean' and beautiful. These were the same men who were indignant when they saw Jesus eating with sinners:

[1] This is an additional indication that the sending of the 'angels' in Mt 24 could well designate the 'mission' of the Church.
[2] The whole fourteenth chapter of Luke contains several lessons taught by Christ about the assembly: De Meeus, La composition de Lc. 14. Eph. Lov. Th. 1961, pp. 847–870.

And the scribes of the Pharisees, when they saw that he was eating with sinners and tax collectors, said to his disciples, 'Why does he eat with tax collectors and sinners?' And when Jesus heard it, he said to them, 'Those who are well have no need of a physician, but those who are sick; I came not to call the righteous, but the sinners' (Mk 2:16–17).

The Christian assembly is certainly not just a gathering together of sinners. Its activity transformed them and clothed them with a wedding garment. It is also established that the summons to the assembly was clearly addressed to sinners and publicans.

There were other social categories which, while not absolutely rejected from the Jewish assembly, were admitted only on a lower level; these Christ also invited to the new assembly. This applied especially to women and children. The rabbinic regulations about them are well known:

All are obliged to appear before God, except the deaf, the idiot and the young, any man with malformed organs, androgynous, women, unfreed slaves, the lame, the blind, the sick, the old and those who cannot walk (Hagiga, 1:1; *Textes rabbiniques*, Ed. Bonsirven, no. 1093).

Women, children, slaves are not included among those whom one blesses (Berakot, 7:2; *ibid.*, no. 450).

These prohibitions explain more clearly the meaning of the episodes in Christ's life in which he declares his desire to summon women and children. He is not satisfied with driving the buyers from the Temple and bringing in the blind and the lame, he also brings in the children and scandalises those in charge of the holy place:

But when the chief priests and the scribes saw the wonderful things that he did, and the children crying in the Temple, 'Hosanna to the Son of David!' they were indignant; and they said to him, 'Do you hear what these are saying?' And Jesus said to them, 'Yes; have you not read "Out of the mouths of babes and sucklings thou hast brought perfect praise"?' (Mt 21:15–16).

The full meaning of other episodes can be understood much more clearly when they are read in the light of the new doctrine of the assembly:

Then children were brought to him that he might lay his hands on them and pray. The disciples rebuked the people, but Jesus said, 'Let the children come to me, and do not hinder them; for to such belongs the kingdom of heaven' (Mt 19:13–14).

To the question whether women can take part in the Christian assembly, Luke answers by multiplying accounts of Christ's interventions on their behalf. This is especially true in the case of the sinful woman present at the meal offered to Jesus by the Pharisee (Lk 7:36–50). This account is followed immediately by the list of the women who devoted themselves to the service of the Lord (Lk 8:1–4); and the case of the crippled woman who was cured right in the middle of the synagogal assembly (Lk 13:10–13).

The assembly summoned by Christ is, therefore, open to all and in this universalism finds its true role. While the new assembly is presented as the meeting of all, most of the gospel texts mention one or other of Christ's interventions against Jewish prohibitions or particularism. Thus the account of his introduction of children and the lame into the Temple follows its purification. The incident of the Canaanite woman and the crumbs of bread dropped from the table follows a discussion of the clean and unclean. The summoning of pagans to the assembly does not really take place until after the destruction of Jerusalem and its Temple:

... the hour is coming when neither on this mountain nor in Jerusalem will you worship the Father . . . the true worshippers will worship the Father in spirit and truth . . . (Jn 4:21, 23).

But if Christ abolished the Jewish regulations limiting the number of men summoned to the assembly, what did he put in their place? How was the call made and how was it answered? The abundance of relevant facts supplied by the gospel is an indication that the first Christian assemblies spent a long time searching for new criteria in these matters.

As a conclusion to these remarks about Christ's intention to summon everyone to the assembly, we can consider for a moment the way Matthew writes about the Sermon on the Mount. Obviously the evangelist wished to make it the Christian counterpart to the Sinai assembly. The crowds came together (Mt 5:1 contrary to Lk 6:20) and the Lord gave his new law just as Moses did the old law (Mt 5:17–26; 6) and instead of the famous curses of Deut 27:14–26, he proposed as a profession of faith the Beatitudes which are as many invitations to the poor and the unclean.

But when he came down from the mountain actually to call the new assembly together, just as Moses had summoned the old one, in succession Christ cured a leper (Mt 8:1–4), a pagan (Mt 8:5–13), and a woman (Mt 8:11–15), three representatives of categories excluded from the old Jewish assembly. The evangelist's intention in grouping here three miracles which the other synoptists report in different contexts is clear. A new Sinai has appeared in which the desert assembly rediscovers its constitution through which it is to be especially open to all those who had been excluded under the old system.

A NEW KIND OF CONVOCATION

Unlike the Jewish summons (Num 19:19–20), the Christian summons includes both 'good and bad' (Mt 22:10). This lack of discrimination must have created a problem in the first Christian communities, but Christ's teaching on this point was so explicit that there was no mistaking his thought. Besides the parable of the wedding feast, where the 'good and bad' were invited, we have the parable of the net and the darnel which are both centred on the 'gathering together': *synagōgē* (Mt 13:30, 47). Jesus related these parables at a moment in his life when the crowds were beginning to leave him and when his enemies were growing in number. The apostles who remained faithful rebelled against this kind of treachery and wished that a sign from heaven would clearly separate the good from the bad:

The servants said to him, 'Then do you want us to go and gather them?' (Mt 13:28).

But Jesus' answer was clear:

Let both grow together until the harvest; and at harvest time I will tell the reapers, Gather the weeds first and bind them in bundles to be burned, but gather the wheat into my barn (Mt 13:30).[1]

The same lesson is taught in the parable of the net:

Again, the kingdom of heaven is like a net which is thrown into the sea and gathered fish of every kind; when it was full, men drew it ashore and sat down and sorted the good into vessels but threw away the bad (Mt 13:47–48).[2]

The gathering together, therefore, will take place in two phases. Here the missionary is invited to bring together the good and the bad, the good grain and the weeds, and to gather on the shore 'all manner of things without any kind of discrimination or judgment'.[3] Not till the second stage will God pronounce a judgment that will separate the good from the bad.

This is a marked change from the Jewish convocation which considered itself fully qualified both to assemble and to judge; Christ, on the other hand, called on the missionary to speak to all men, excluding no one *a priori*. He wished the missionary to play a pastoral role which would rally all men, leaving until a later time the work of judging and separating. This is the lesson of the parable of the feast. The servants are asked to invite without discrimination everyone they meet, good and bad, in the streets and the highways. The master of the household reserves to himself the right to judge and to exclude:

. . . and he said to him, 'Friend, how did you get in here without a wedding garment?' And he was speechless. Then the king said to the attendants, 'Bind him hand and foot, and cast him into the outer darkness; there men weep and gnash their teeth' (Mt 22:12–13).

In these words the mission of those charged with the summons to the assembly is clearly stated: All men are called. The message must be sufficiently universal for all men to respond to it and for all social classes to understand it. It should be so inspired by love

---

[1] Exegesis of this parable in Mouson, *Explicatur parabola de zizaniis in agro.* Coll. Mech. 1959, pp. 171–175.

[2] Exegesis in Didier, *Les paraboles de l'ivraie et du filet*, Rev. dioc. Namur 1960, 49119.

[3] An expression no less pejorative expressing the very general nature of the assembly than the 'gather them together' to which Mt 22:10 alludes. (Cf. p. 42)!

and mercy that sinners will feel that the invitation belongs to them just as much as it does to the good. Therefore the mission of him who summons is very different from the role of God whose judgment makes possible this definitive entrance into the Kingdom. Between the time of the first and the second calling, each one must respond.

The concept of time is one of those which best shows the difference between the Jewish and the Christian assembly. Without this concept the Jews confused summons and judgment, and, allowing no delay, at once excluded sinners and unclean. For Christians, on the contrary, in the Kingdom is already realised an anticipation, although an imperfect one, of the definitive assembly. This was based on a summons freed from all restriction and specialisation, leaving to each one time to be converted.

This is not all. The convocation not only allowed an interval for conversion but it effected this conversion by transforming the assembly into one of healing and pardon. We were invited to understand this when we watched Jesus curing a sick man (Mt 21:14), or a crippled woman (Lk 13:10–17), so that they could enter an assembly whose gates hitherto had been closed to them. Or when he forgave a sinful woman at a banquet given by a Pharisee (Lk 7:36–50). The invitation to the assembly offered to the sinner or to the unclean man is matched by the power to pardon and purify. This clarifies another essential difference between the convocation proposed by the Old Testament and the one instituted by Christ. The first, lacking the power to purify, had to exclude the sinner. The second could forgive and therefore could address sinners directly, transforming itself into a place where they could be forgiven and where they could be converted.

Later teaching was to define all that is implied in the relation between convocation and forgiveness by investing the president of the assembly with the necessary jurisdiction to absolve those who had been invited. In this way the Christian assembly, strong in its ability to triumph over sin, could welcome the sinner as long as he was capable of conversion, and could acknowledge him as one of its members. But if the sinner became obdurate, then the assembly made itself responsible for him:

If your brother sins against you, go and tell him his fault, between you and him alone. If he listens to you, you have gained your brother. But if he does not listen, take one or two others along with you, that every word may be confirmed by the evidence of two or three witnesses (see Deut 19:15). But if he refuses to listen to them, tell it to the church; and if he refuses to listen even to the church, let him be to you as a Gentile and a tax collector (Mt 18:15–18).

The lesson of this passage is plain. The Christian will not consider another man to be a pagan or a publican (two categories which were excluded from the Jewish assembly) until after he has tried to convert him by love and mercy.[1]

Responsible for the conversion of the man who knocked at its door, the assembly soon instituted the catechumenate which was devised to verify the candidate's faith and accustom him to community life. It is necessary to wait until the apostolic documents, Acts and epistles, before we find the oldest traces of this discipline, but certain acts and gestures of Christ were quickly interpreted in this sense. The cure of the deaf man (Mk 7:32–33) which precedes the multiplication of the loaves, which recalls the desert assembly and is a symbol of the eucharistic assembly, and the cure of the blind man (Mk 8:22–23) which follows shortly after this incident, are obviously patterned on a catechumenate ritual, as if they were meant to serve as a model for the initiation of any stranger to the eucharistic assembly:

And they brought to him a man who was deaf . . . (Mk 7:32).

And some people brought to him a blind man . . . (Mk 8:22).

'To bring' suggests more than a charitable act. The expression has a technical meaning and denotes the attitude of the guarantors who present a candidate and who recommend him.[2] The rest

---

[1] French translations of the gospels under the influence of theology translate 'Tell it to the Church', instead of 'Tell it to the assembly.' Yet it is clear that the assembly as it was in the early Church had the right to judge the sinner and excommunicate him and enjoyed a power which at the present time is reserved to the hierarchy. Cf. 1 Cor 5:4–8. But today's teaching in no way prevents the local assembly from welcoming the stranger, the questioning of catechumens who present themselves, the assigning of godparents, and so on.

[2] Cf. Thierry Maertens, *Histoire et pastorale du catéchuménat et du baptême* (Coll. Paroisse et Liturgie), Ed. Biblica, 1963, ad loc.

of the account shows clearly that reference is made to some kind of catechumenate: the imposition of hand, the touching of each sense, these days of fasting, etc.

The missionary activity, the temporal value of the summons, the connection between the right to pardon and the assembly, the role of godparents and the catechumenate, all this was already outlined in the earliest theology of the assembly and gave entirely new dimensions to the Christian summons.

THE RISEN ONE, THE CENTRE OF THE CONVOCATION

In the foregoing analysis the conclusion was repeatedly reached that the work of gathering together undertaken by God centres now around the risen Christ who replaces the old Jerusalem. Moreover, the evangelists insist that the Lord's appearances took place in the presence of the assembled disciples:

> . . . and they found the eleven gathered together and those who were with them . . . (Lk 24:33).

> On the evening of that day, the first day of the week, the doors being shut . . . where the disciples were (Jn 20:19).[1]

> Eight days later, his disciples were again in the house (Jn 20:26).

> So when they had come together they questioned him . . . (Acts 1:6).

> When the day of Pentecost had come, they were all together in one place . . . (Acts 2:1).

It is fairly easy to identify the sources which tell of assemblies or gatherings around the presence of the risen Christ. Some came from John who is the most theological and most sacramentally-minded of the evangelists. Some also came from Luke, or at least from sources used by him. Schools of exegetes admit that St Luke drew inspiration from sources coming from circles faithful to the 'Twelve', but he knew how to modify their facts according to information received from the circle devoted to the disciples (the account of the Lord's appearance to the disciples of Emmaus) and through information furnished by Hellenistic circles in the

[1] The word 'assembly' is found in some manuscripts.

Jewish community. These testimonies stand out. To a concept of
a Temple-centred assembly (Lk 24:51–53) cherished by Judaeo-
Christians is contrasted the more spiritualised concept of an
assembly in whose midst is the majestic presence of the Risen
One.

Luke and John, moving away from apologetic goals and less
concerned about the past, look upon the resurrection as an event
establishing new structures. Thus the appearances of Christ took
place not in private, as if they were merely proofs of his resurrection, but in an assembly as if to establish more definitely the
assemblies of the future.[1]

But why does Christ not appear in assembly with his disciples
until after his resurrection? This question can be answered only
by analysing the content of each of these assemblies in which
the Lord was present. One by one we shall take elements from
the old Jewish assembly and compare them with elements that
appeared in the assemblies of the Lord. We can thus measure the
distance we have covered.

In the Old Testament, God summoned his own people through
the king or the priests. After the resurrection the convocation is
even more startling. The Lord himself appears in the midst of his
own. The assembly is, therefore, more than ever the fruit of
divine initiative. It is not the act of men who try to measure up
to the demands of the virtue of religion by rendering worship to
their God. It is the fruit of an initiative by God who manifests
himself to his own. The strongest justification for the assembly is
more than ever due to God's initiative.

A second important element of the Jewish assembly and one
which is also found in the Lord's assemblies, is the proclamation
of the Word. We can take as an example the assembly that the
Lord arranged with the disciples of Emmaus:

> And beginning with Moses and the prophets, he interpreted to them
> in all the scriptures the things concerning himself (Lk 24:27).

Or the Easter Sunday evening assembly with the apostles:

> '. . . everything written about me in the law of Moses and the

---

[1] It does not concern us that the mention of the assembly in Jn 20:19 may be
derived from a later tradition, as some evidence taken from the texts suggests.

prophets and the psalms must be fulfilled.' Then he opened their minds to understand the scriptures (Lk 24:44–45).

In the Jewish assembly, the Word recalled the conditions of the covenant and prepared for its renewal. In the new assembly, the Word led the disciples from unbelief to real faith in the presence of the Risen Lord. Thus the assembly is the place where faith is experienced, where man learns to transcend sensible experience to attain a knowledge of Christ the Lord. The man who is summoned is not necessarily a believer; each time, in a certain sense, he must reconquer his faith. He is one of those who are:

. . . foolish men, and slow of heart to believe all that the prophets have spoken (Lk 24:25).

The story of doubting Thomas is significant in this respect (Jn 20:24–28). As long as the man who comes into the assembly relies only on sense-knowledge and on human methods of investigation, he misses the essential:

. . . Have you believed because you have seen me? Blessed is he who has not seen and yet believes (Jn 20:29).

Therefore, the new assembly has a content that can be grasped only by faith, a faith awakened and trained by the initiative of God's Word. But it is exactly here that the assembly held in the presence of the Lord introduces something new. Unlike the proclamation of the Word in Jewish assemblies which always looked to the past or pointed to a distant future, the proclamation that our Lord made in the assemblies that he called is a fulfilment (Lk 24:44); his own person is the key opening men's minds to an understanding of the Scriptures (Lk 24:45). After all to inaugurate his ministry, he himself commented upon a reading made during a sabbath assembly in the following simple words:

Today this scripture has been fulfilled in your hearing (Lk 4:21).

We can understand how the disciples at Emmaus felt when they heard him explain the 'fulfilment' of the Scriptures:

Did not our hearts burn within us while he talked to us on the road while he opened to us the scriptures? (Lk 24:32).

This presence of the Lord which, in the sacramental rite, 'dwells' in every assembly, is entirely original and did not appear in the old system of assembly. When the risen Lord gathers his own around him in the assembly, his intention is to initiate them in the exercise of his powers of lordship which he entrusted specifically to the assemblies. In this way from the first day of his appearances the Lord hands over to his own the power to forgive sins:

> If you forgive the sins of any, they are forgiven; if you retain the sins of any, they are retained (Jn 20:23).

This power is not merely the sacramental forgiveness of penance but also of baptising (also remission of sins, cf. Acts 2:38) and to make the Eucharist (also 'for the remission of sins' cf. Mt 26:28). In other words, Christ, who triumphed over death and sin, gave similar powers to the assemblies that met in his name. The assembled Christians have conquered sin and their very assembly brings into their midst the risen Lord with all his lordly prerogatives. He who took the initiative of summoning the assemblies of the new covenant no longer fears sin because he has triumphed over it in his resurrection and does not cease to triumph by summoning sinners, through his ministers, to the new assembly.

Moreover, other lordly powers were distributed and exercised in the assemblies held after the resurrection. Thus Peter received the mandate 'to feed my sheep' (Jn 21:15–17), a mandate connected even in the Old Testament with the mission of gathering together.[1]

But the most profound of all signs of the Lord's presence in the midst of the assembly is the Eucharist. It was during a eucharistic meal that the disciples at Emmaus recognised him:[2]

> When he was at table with them he took the bread and blessed, and broke it, and gave it to them. And their eyes were opened and they recognised him . . . he was known to them in the breaking of the bread (Lk 24:30–31, 35).

---

[1] Cf. p. 40.

[2] This is the theme of 'knowledge' which is no longer simple human knowledge, just as Christ was known before his resurrection, but faith which is needed to understand the meaning of every assembly.

There is the same passing from incomprehension to understanding in the assembly gathered on the shores of the lake of
Tiberias in a rite that, at the very least, recalls the eucharistic
meal:

Jesus said to them, 'Come and have breakfast.' Now none of the
disciples dared ask him, 'Who are you?' They knew it was the Lord.
Jesus came and took the bread and gave it to them . . . (Jn 21:12–13).

On several occasions the risen Lord expressed his desire to
assemble his own at a meal (Acts 1:4; Lk 24:41). This desire was
much less evident before his passion and resurrection. So that he
might always be in the midst of those whom he summoned he
established a ritual meal, the expression of the assembly of all
men in one spirit.

Thus the Lord introduced a new kind of assembly centred
around himself, not in the Temple but in faith and through the
exercise of a series of lordly powers which he placed at the dis-
position of the Christian assembly: victory over sin, hierarchy
which is the visible sign of assembly, eucharistic meal which is
the expression of this assembly. Superimposed upon the Temple
rites are new, more spiritual, signs which can only be deciphered
after a continuing initiation in the faith, but which are 'in truth'
signs of the Lord's presence in the midst of his own, as assembler
of his people.

After the proclamation of the Word and the celebration of the
rite, there is a third constituent element, the sending on a mission.
Almost all the meetings with the risen Lord conclude with the
apostles and disciples being sent on a mission to assemble the
nations. The Christians gathered round the Lord in their turn call
others to the assembly:

As the Father has sent me, even so I send you (Jn 20:21).

Mark is even more explicit:

And he said to them, 'Go into all the world and preach the gospel to
the whole creation' (Mk 16:15).

John lays particular emphasis on this missionary implication of
the Lord's appearances to his own. Thus in Chapter 21, the

assembly of the apostles on the shores of Lake Genesareth coincides with the miraculous catch of one hundred and fifty-three fish (Jn 21:6–11), probably a symbol of the assembly of the whole world in the Kingdom (Mt 4:19; 13:47). If we accept the hypothesis that one hundred and fifty-three species of fish were known at that time, then this number denotes the whole kingdom of fish, a token of the universal gathering of all men in the nets of the apostles.

The last meeting that the Lord held with his disciples before Pentecost was again marked by the sending of its members to the whole world:

> ... You shall be my witnesses in Jerusalem and in all Judea and Samaria and to the end of the earth (Acts 1:8).

There is a final characteristic to be noted. These gatherings of the disciples round the risen Christ took place on a Sunday. We owe the accounts of these Sunday appearances especially to John:

> On the evening of that day, the first day of the week, the doors being shut where the disciples were for fear of the Jews, Jesus came and stood among them ... (Jn 20:19).

And the following Sunday:

> Eight days later, his disciples were again in the house, and Thomas was with them. The doors were shut, but Jesus came and stood among them ... (Jn 20:26).

The last appearance of the Lord closed with the sending of the Holy Spirit. This assembly took place on Pentecost Sunday:

> When the day of Pentecost had come, they were all together in one place (Acts 2:1).

It is perhaps not impossible that the same teaching about Sunday emerges in another passage of St John (Jn 1:19–22; 12) where, at the close of a whole week entirely consecrated to the 'calling' of his own, the Lord assembled them at Cana, and there performed the first sign of his glory.

The time between Easter and Pentecost, therefore, was for the first disciples a period of initiation during which, from Sunday to

Sunday, they learned to cleanse their minds so that they can recognise the risen Lord present among them in increasingly spiritual form. By means of this chronological information, John wished to turn on the Sunday assemblies of the first Christians the same light that came from the assemblies of the risen Lord with his apostles. These are the moments in which the presence of the Lord in the midst of his own is experienced in faith through the Word, the rites, the messianic powers and the missionary mandate.

The information furnished by the description of the risen Lord's assemblies enables a doctrine of assembly to be formulated which can be summarised at this point.

First of all, the assembly is closely connected with the resurrection. Before this event no mention is ever made of the assembly. If John alludes to it at the miracle of Cana it is only because he sees in it an anticipatory sign of the glory of the Lord. Further, during the short interval between his passover and his ascension, the risen Lord had no other desire than the initiation of his own in this new kind of assembly, so different from what they would have known both from the Temple and the synagogue liturgy.

If our Lord claimed the right of summoning an assembly, it was because his resurrection made him the master of the world 'to unite all things in him, things in heaven and things on earth' (Eph 1:9–10). The missionary mandate given to those who took part in the assembly appeared thereafter as the progressive realisation of the assembly of all creation under the dominion of the risen Lord and the assembly as the sign, in time, of Jesus' dominion over the universe. Therefore, the liturgical assembly, the dominion of Christ and the apostolic mission are clearly related; the assembly is the special time for the intensification of the extension of Christ's dominion over the world. We are far from a simple meeting for worship or presence at a ceremony or even from a community whose bonds were solely psychological or sociological.

The fact that the new assembly gathers in the presence of the risen Lord may explain certain rather strange attitudes of Christ towards the pagans before his rescurrection. For example, addressing the Canaanite woman, he exclaimed:

¹ See p. 21.

It is not fair to take the children's bread and throw it to the dogs (Mt 15:26).

Some Jews remained much too faithful to this severity and so the evangelists felt it necessary to place this episode in the general context of Christ's teaching. More correctly than Matthew (15:21–22), Mark situates it on pagan territory (7:24) and for the allusion to the masters substitutes the less humiliating allusion to children (Mk 7:28). Finally, Mark and Matthew insert this episode in a catechumenical and eucharistic context (Mk 6:30–38; 26) emphasising the element of initiation into the assembly rather than that of exclusion.

The episode of the sellers expelled from the Temple, in which Christ threw down the barriers preventing the summons from being addressed to all, might equally be an indication of Christ's will to summon pagans. Did not the Second Zechariah see this in advance as a sign of the welcome of all nations to Jerusalem?

> Then every one that survives of all the nations that have come against Jerusalem shall go up year after year to worship the King, the Lord of hosts, and to keep the feast of booths . . . And there shall no longer be a trader in the house of the Lord of hosts on that day (Zech 14:16–21).

But Jesus did not connect his act with this prophecy of a universal assembly. And in addition, he left out the second part of the quotation of Isaiah 56:7. 'My house will be called a house of prayer for *all peoples*!' Does this mean that Christ who came to bring all men together does not want pagans to be welcomed to his assembly? On the contrary, it is enough to re-read his eschatological discourse (Mt 24) or Luke's banquet parable (Lk 14:16–24) to realise this, but he places the assembly of the nations after the destruction of the city or of the Temple of Jerusalem. The historical Christ still bound to the forms of Jewish messianism cannot bring about this assembly. The mystical Christ, the risen Lord, alone can do this because he now possesses the right to call upon the whole world.[1]

> . . . And I, when I am lifted up from the earth, will draw all men to myself (Jn 12:32).

[1] See p. 71.

This last assertion is all the more enlightening because it is the answer to Philip's request on behalf of the pagans who wished to meet Christ (Jn 12:20–23). This encounter will be possible, Jesus declared, only after his glorification and his establishment 'on the clouds coming in power and glory' (Mt 24:30).

The accounts of the Lord's ascension also connect his entrance into glory with the universal mission of the disciples:

> So then the Lord Jesus, after he had spoken to them, was taken up into heaven, and sat down at the right hand of God. And they went forth and preached everywhere, while the Lord worked with them and confirmed the message by the signs that attended (Mk 16:19–20).

In the assembly instituted by Christ for all men, the pagans were also included but perhaps for them, more than for all others, their being called depended on the glory acquired by the risen Lord.

CONCLUSION

In ancient Israel the summons to the assembly depended on God's personal initiative. Today the development of the assembly is centred on the person of the Lord whose life, attitudes and sentiments it shares in spirit and in truth. It is no longer necessary to belong to a certain culture or to adopt a certain religious ritual. Whoever is able to make his attitudes and sentiments like those of the Lord can share wholly in lordship over the world and its assemblies. Only those men can be excluded from this assembly whom sin deprives of the spiritual attitudes necessary for sharing the lordship of Christ. He gives this assembly the power of triumphing over sin. The convocation turns into pardon when it reaches a sinner, or into healing when it reaches a cripple. Only the hardened sinner is kept at a distance.

This is why the assembly must be a powerful force and why it must allow the universal assembly to develop. Its periodical recurrence on Sunday is a first expression of this eschatological power. The local weekly assembly does not bring together a closed world, a definitive people of the redeemed. It is not a successful achievement but only a sign. It is not an end or a goal but only a stage on the way. This is the reason for its recurrence until the day when the sign will give place to the reality. The Christian assembly is essentially linked with the concept of the time of the Church. It is part of history in process. It can allow itself to summon sinners because they still have time to be converted and to believe. Its essentially missionary character also expresses its eschatological power. The assembly is in fact only a people who have come together to answer God's call in Jesus Christ. Since this call is universal, the assembly is only able to understand itself to the extent that it knows that it is addressed to men and is always catholic. Thus it is indeed the 'sign of the Son of Man coming on the clouds'.

The disciples, going from their regular assemblies in the temple or synagogue to their mysterious meetings with the risen Lord, even continuing for a while to be present at both kinds of assembly, must have gradually come to realise that what formed the difference between them was the presence of the Lord.

This presence first showed itself in the appearances of the risen Lord. These appearances were still physical but very different from the apostles' experience of Christ before his passion. Did they not have to learn to pass from a physical presence in order to realise the reality of a spiritual presence perceived in faith? The gift of the Spirit on Pentecost Sunday ratified this lesson. Ever since that day the members of the assembly were able to recognise the Lord in his signs and to live by his presence.

This presence is to be found in the Word which is no longer merely the simple account of past events or the programme of a distant and inaccessible future but is its accomplishment here and now in the assembly. It is also to be grasped in the rite that communicates the very life of the Lord and his messianic powers. This new mode of presence profoundly troubled the disciples. When the evangelists mention the apostles' doubts, fright or hestitations when they saw the risen Lord, they are telling us that the appearances found the apostles unprepared; consequently these appearances are not the creation of their disappointed imagination. Moreover, insisting on the disappointment of the apostles who were awaiting the Lord's presence as a kind of 'recovery' of the old presence and who had to accustom their eyes and their minds to a new mode of presence (the presence of the Lord in the rites and in the community itself), the accounts of the appearances were trying to describe the process of faith necessary for participation in the assembly and the obligatory initiation of each one into this new mode of presence. This presence is not to be perceived on the material or the earthly level but on the level of signs. Christians assemble not merely to recall the historic Christ but to meet Christ the Lord who made use of the elements of the world he rules to signify his presence. This is why the assembly-sign cannot be perceived by the virtue of religion alone. It must be crowned by faith if the Lord is to be recognised. This initiation in faith should be renewed each time, otherwise the assembly will be no more than a single manifestation of piety and religion and will contain many a doubting Thomas who will be satisfied with sensible and sentimental expressions and who will completely miss the real meaning of the assembly.

3

The first Christian assemblies[1]

—∿∿ΩΩ◉ΩΩ∿∿—

[1] Henri Chirat, L'Assemblée chrétienne à l'âge apostolique (*Lex orandi series, 10*), Paris, 1949, is still the basic historical work in the field. But I think that a new point of view may serve to reinforce some of the author's analyses.

WHILE THE EVANGELISTS on the basis of Christ's actions were fashioning the charter of the new assembly, in the midst of their difficulties the first Christian communities were making every effort to observe it. The Acts of the Apostles and the letters of St Paul show us how the fundamental principles of the assembly were gradually laid down and how this led to several crises which even today affect our own assemblies.

THE JERUSALEM ASSEMBLY

The Jerusalem community was the first to encounter the problems of the meaning and the structure of the assembly. Fifty days after the Lord's passover, the community was already established and was at once confronted abruptly with reality. Yet only gradually was it able to meet these problems with the best possible solutions in keeping with the mind of the Lord.

THE FEAST OF PENTECOST

In the days of Christ Judaism looked on Pentecost as the commemoration of the assembly of the people on Sinai. On this feast in the year 30, the apostles met 'all together' in 'one place' (Acts 2:1) in keeping with contemporary Jewish custom, or even with the regulations of some sect, the Essenes or some other. Probably they reflected on the circumstances of the first Sinai assembly,[1] an event long since past but which they expected would now be renewed as the prophets had foretold.[2]

[1] There is a hint of this in the fact that Peter in his discourses alluded to Ps 68 which was one of the psalms of this feast.
[2] For the exegesis of this difficult chapter (Acts 2) see Sabbe, *Het Pinksterverhaal,* Coll. Brug. Gand. 1957, pp. 161–178.

And so they began to understand that their meeting was the assembly that had been foreseen by the prophets, and this belief was confirmed by the repetition of certain of the natural phenomena similar to those which had taken place on Sinai.

And suddenly a sound came from heaven like the rush of a mighty wind, and it filled all the house where they were sitting. And there appeared to them tongues as of fire, distributed and resting on each of them. And they were all filled with the Holy Spirit and began to speak in other tongues, as the Spirit gave them utterance (Acts 2:2–4).

The description of the Exodus had told them:

. . . there were thunders and lightnings, and a thick cloud upon the mountain, and a very loud trumpet blast, so that all the people who were in the camp trembled . . . And Mount Sinai was wrapped in smoke, because the Lord descended upon it in fire . . . (Exod 19:16, 18).

Now when all the people perceived the thunderings and the lightnings and the sound of the trumpet and the mountain smoking, the people were afraid and trembled . . . (Exod 20:18).

When the rabbis commented on these texts they readily agreed that God spoke in the fire. It is likely that it was this association between the Word and the flame that the apostles recalled when they alluded to 'the tongues as of fire' that came down on each one and made their gathering the new covenant assembly. But if they knew that their little assembly on Zion was the replica of the great assembly on Sinai, they also believed that it possessed the characteristics of the eschatological assembly, especially the gathering together of all nations. Interpreting the phenomenon of glossolalia that seized them, they wished to see in it the special charism that made their meeting the assembly of the nations:

Now there were dwelling in Jerusalem Jews, devout men from every nation under heaven. And at this sound the multitude came together, and they were bewildered, because each one heard them speaking in his own language. And they were amazed and wondered, saying, 'Are not all these who are speaking Galileans? And how is it that we hear, each of us in his own native language? Parthians and Medes and Elamites and residents of Mesopotamia, Judea and Cappadocia,

Pontus and Asia, Phrygia and Pamphylia, Egypt and the parts of Libya belonging to Cyrene, and visitors from Rome, both Jews and proselytes, Cretans and Arabians, we hear them telling in our own tongues the mighty works of God (Acts 2:5–11).

A SOCIOLOGICAL ASSEMBLY OF THE POOR

The Jerusalem community did not know how to realise in suitable form this knowledge that they were part of the assembly foretold by the prophets. Nevertheless they began to carry out thoroughgoing reforms. Thus the Christians of the city abolished the prohibitions and divisions that had afflicted the Jewish assembly. James himself, who was responsible for the community, invited everyone:

> My brethren, show no partiality as you hold the faith of our Lord Jesus Christ, the Lord of glory. For if a man with gold rings and in fine clothing comes into your assembly, and a poor man in shabby clothing also comes in, and you pay attention to the one who wears the fine clothing and say, 'Have a seat here, please,' while you say to the poor man, 'Stand there,' or 'Sit at my feet,' have you not made distinctions among yourselves and become judges with evil thoughts? (Jas 2:1–4).

Luke reported with enthusiasm the inner unity of this community:

> And they devoted themselves to the apostles' teaching and fellowship, to the breaking of bread and the prayers. And fear came upon every soul; and many wonders and signs were done through the apostles. And all who believed were together and had all things in common; and they sold their possessions and goods and distributed them to all, as any had need (Acts 2:42–45; see also Acts 1:13–14; 4:33–37; 5:12).

More plainly than in the Jewish assemblies, the poor became the members *par excellence* of the Christian assemblies in Jerusalem. So true was this that the rich, in order to take part, had to sell all their goods and make themselves like the poor in their material destitution. Luke entered so profoundly into this doctrine of material poverty which was necessary for entrance into the Kingdom (Lk 6:20, 24; 12:13–34; 14:28–33; 16:9, 19–31; 18:18–

30; 19:8–9) that we have a fairly exact picture of the concept of absolute detachment that inspired the primitive Jerusalem assembly. Brutal excommunication and death were the hard sanctions incurred by the rich man who wanted to keep for himself some part of his own possessions (Acts 5).

The Jerusalem assembly was probably among those who gave a strictly sociological meaning to the Beatitudes announced by Christ:

> Blessed are you poor, for yours is the kingdom of God.
> Blessed are you that hunger now, for you shall be satisfied.
> Blessed are you that weep now, for you shall laugh (Lk 6:20–21).

A too narrow understanding of these Beatitudes would suggest that an invitation to the Kingdom and membership would automatically follow for those who were poor, who wept, who were hungry, or who faced persecution.[1] This is the same mistake as that made by the servants in the parable of the darnel. They were sent to invite, they tried to judge and discriminate. The parable of the wedding garment and the nuances introduced in the Beatitudes by Matthew show that, although the poor are indeed invited, the assembly cannot allow itself to be absorbed by any social category, not even by the poor!

However attractive this offer to the poor may appear to be, it may be wondered whether it is in conformity with the demands laid down by Christ for the assembly of the last days. This assembly would have to stay above sociological groups and human categories, thus accustoming all social classes to live in community, yet without at the same time reducing them all to one class. Actually, the rich had to make themselves sociologically poor (Acts 4:32, 36–37) to deserve to take part in the assembly. Far from making this a sign of the universal assembly, the assembly is seen to be bound up exclusively with a given social class.

In the assembly, the poor, avenging themselves on the rich, seized the Kingdom for themselves and reduced the universalist

---

[1] See J. Dupont, *Les Béatitudes*, 2nd edn, D.D.B. 1961. It is clear that Luke, both in his gospel and in Acts, was reporting certain traditions proper to the Jerusalem community while the other synoptics corrected or spiritualised more than Luke. See Staudinger, *Testis primarius évangélii sec. Lucam*, Verb. Dom. 1955, pp. 129–142.

significance of the assembly to their own concept of class. The Jerusalem assembly became so poor that help from all the assemblies of converts from paganism was needed to lift them out of their misery (Rom 15:26–28; 1 Cor 16:1–3; 2 Cor 8–9). Taught by this experience, Matthew did not hesitate to correct the interpretation of the Beatitudes revealed by the practice of the Christians of Jerusalem. He suppressed every allusion to the woes pronounced against the rich (Lk 6:24) and speaks rather of the poor 'in spirit' (Mt 5:3). Of couse it is true that the Church must be open to the unfortunate and has never been so sufficiently. It is indeed true that the poor are most loved by God, but the ideal of the assembly is not realised by reducing its recruitment to one class. From the doctrinal viewpoint, it would be just as serious to transform our own assemblies into gatherings of the middle class as it would be to transform them into gatherings of the poor. One or the other would become a ghetto and a closed community, thus losing their meaning as signs denoting the purpose of the assembly that our Lord laid upon his Church.

Open to the poor, the Jerusalem assembly was also open to categories excommunicated in previous assemblies. Thus the lame were openly made welcome:

> And he took him by the right hand and raised him up; and immediately his feet and ankles were made strong. And leaping up he stood and walked and entered the temple with them, walking and leaping and praising God (Acts 3:7–8).

Peter's first miracle, therefore, reproduced for the lame man the summons to the assembly that Christ had already shown them when he brought the lame into the Temple assembly (Mt 21:14–15).[1] We know that Peter, like Christ, was arrested by the Sanhedrin precisely because he had disregarded this prohibition.

Philip, in his turn, was to abolish another prohibition when he brought Queen Candace's eunuch into the Church (Acts 8:26–38) in spite of the very clear regulation of the Jewish law about those 'unclean' persons (Deut 23:2).

The first Christians of Jerusalem understood Christ's intention about the assembly. They wanted to be true 'assemblers' of

[1] See the commentary on p. 41.

men who had previously been excluded; but unfortunately they succeeded in assembling only one social class.

OUTMODED MEANS OF ASSEMBLY

For the Christians of Jerusalem, the centre of the assembly was still the Temple of Mount Zion. Was it not around this mount that the prophets had proclaimed the assembly of Jewish tribes and the nations? These Christians had not yet understood that Christ's risen body had been substituted for the Temple as the centre of the assembly.

It is sufficient to read again St Luke's account of our Lord's ascension (Lk 24:50–53) to appreciate the importance of the Temple and the city of Jerusalem in the piety of the first Christians:

> And they worshipped him, and returned to Jerusalem with great joy, and were continually in the temple blessing God (Lk 24:52–53).

This conclusion is at variance with those completing the other accounts of the ascension – including the one Luke placed at the beginning of his book of Acts – directed no longer towards the Temple but to the universal mission of the Church. The Jerusalem Christians must, therefore, have been convinced that the glorification of Zion would follow the Lord's ascension because they insisted so strongly on the order given by the Lord to the apostles that they should remain in Jerusalem and await this apotheosis:

> . . . but stay in the city, until you are clothed with power from on high (Lk 24:49).

The assiduous attendance of the apostles and the Christians of Jerusalem in the Zion Temple was, moreover, one of the characteristics of the first community:

> And day by day, attending the temple together . . . (Acts 2:46).

The apostles went to the Temple to take part in the evening sacrifice (Acts 3:1), or to teach in the porches (Acts 5:25) just as Christ himself had done (Lk 19:47). In their defence it must be admitted that they did not yet possess very clear teaching on the content of the Christian sacrifice. Why should this surprise us

when Paul himself, before he had definitely formulated his theology of spiritual worship and the Christian assembly, felt himself
obliged to go to the Temple to alleviate the susceptibilities of the
Jerusalem Christians?[1]

> Then Paul took the men, and the next day he purified himself with
> them and went into the temple, to give notice when the days of
> purification would be fulfilled and the offering presented for every
> one of them (Acts 21:26).

This exclusive concentration on the Temple was especially
true of the Hebrews, that is to say, of the Palestinian Jews who
had become Christians and who were far more strongly attached
to the Temple than were the disciples who came from the Jewish
diaspora and, *a fortiori*, the Christians converted from paganism.
But how could the Hebrews pretend to assemble all men and
all cultures around a particular form of worship, with rites and
ceremonies proper to one nation? A religion claiming to assemble
all men must be able to put before them a worship with a
sufficiently spiritual content to find a place in every form of life
and culture. But despite efforts of spiritualisation already accepted
under the influence of the prophets, the Temple cult had never
been able to free itself from local customs (Mt 1:6–12; 6). The
failure to realise this was the weakness of the first Christian
assembly in Jerusalem.

But other assemblies, similar to those of the Temple, took
place in Jerusalem. Luke, describing the primitive community in
Acts 2:46–47,[2] speaks not only of the Temple cult but also of
worship in 'houses' in which the first Christians took their meals
according to the Jewish custom of the breaking of bread. The
few hints found in Acts suggest that these house assemblies
consisted of Christians who had belonged to the diaspora or who
had been pagans. This is true of the house of John Mark's family
(Acts 12:12) where Peter went after he left prison.

---

[1] It must be admitted, in Paul's defence, that he took advantage of this sad
Jerusalem visit to raise again the problem of the pagans meeting in the temple:
'he also brought the Greeks into the temple' (Acts 21:28). Even though un-
justified, this accusation brings us back to the assembly theme. It led to Paul's
condemnation just as it did to that of Jesus, Peter and Stephen (Mt 26:61;
Acts 4:7–11; 6:14).

[2] See *infra*, p. 70.

When Christians organised these assemblies in private houses, they were putting forward a formula singularly more universalist than that found in the Temple liturgy, for it is much easier to unite men in a brotherly meal than in a Temple ritual. This contrast between private houses and the Temple may have influenced the writing of the gospels. Did Christ not go to a private house after causing uproar in the Temple (Mt 21:17)? And did not the Magi, who came to the Jerusalem Temple carrying the gold and incense foretold in Isa 60:6, find the Assembler in a private house (Mt 2:1–11)? If the annunciation of John the Baptist is made in the Temple (Lk 1:5–23), that of Jesus takes place in a house (Lk 1:26–38). To celebrate the Passover, Christ and his disciples enter a mysterious private house (Mk 14:12–16) at the hour when preparations for the feast were being celebrated in the Temple. Going into the dwelling of Zachaeus, Christ praised this house and called it God's dwelling and the place of salvation, privileges hitherto exclusively reserved for the Temple itself (Lk 19:5–10). As we shall see later, Matthew contrasts the Temple (Mt 21:12–17) with the banquet hall (Mt 22:1–14) as the place of assembly. It should also be pointed out that although Luke concludes his gospel with a description of the meeting of the first Christians in the Temple (Lk 24:53), he closes Acts with a description of the welcome given to all in Paul's house (Acts 28:30). John himself, though writing several years later, still seems aware of this idea because he places the account of the wedding celebration in the house at Cana (Jn 2:1–11) side by side with the account of the Lord's purification of the Temple (Jn 2:13–22).

The failure of the Hebrews in Jerusalem is repeated in all our Christian assemblies when they take the means for the end. It is the failure of Christians, attached to formalistic practices, who can think of the conversion of non-Christians only in terms of their adopting those some practices. It is the failure of Christians, comfortably settled in their good faith, who can only imagine the conversion of the communist world as the rejection of all its principles, without ever wondering whether the Christian world should not take a step towards those whom it is called to convert by stripping itself of certain outmoded forms of thought and

worship. Has it ground for complaint against Jerusalem for mis-
understanding the requirements of its function of a universal
assembly when today so many Christians and communities are
still unable to find such an assembly, and when canon law
defends rubrics and ritual so forcefully that it is impossible for a
westernised liturgy to gather together effectively peoples of Asia
and Africa, or even more simply and immediately the various
cultures and environments that make up every parish?

A TOO JEWISH HIERARCHY[1]

From the first, the apostolic college appears as the most important
organ of the Jerusalem assembly. One hundred and twenty
persons already gathered around the 'Twelve' after the Lord's
ascension (Acts 1:15) and were probably still with them at
Pentecost (Acts 2:1). The 'Twelve' stood themselves as witnesses
to Christ, witnesses who, during his whole life, had watched him
and heard him and who were now telling the disciples what they
must do in order to imitate the Lord (Acts 2:42).

> So one of the men who have accompanied us during all the time that
> the Lord Jesus went in and out among us, beginning from the
> baptism of John until the day when he was taken up from us – one of
> these men must become with us a witness to his resurrection (Acts
> 1:21–22).

The apostles as witnesses of the resurrection gave their
testimony both by their preaching (Acts 2:22–24; 32; 5:29–32),
and by their miraculous powers which proved to the faithful that
the Lord had become the master of the elements of the world:

> Now many signs and wonders were done among the people by the
> hands of the apostles ... so that they even carried out the sick into
> the streets and laid them on beds and pallets, that as Peter came by at
> least his shadow might fall on some of them. The people also gathered
> from the towns around Jerusalem, bringing the sick and those afflicted
> with unclean spirits, and they were all healed (Acts 5:12, 15–16; see
> also Acts 4:33).

The first primitive assembly met round this group of witnesses,

---

[1] Colson, *Les fonctions ecclésiales aux premiers siècles*, D.D.B., Bruges 1956,
pp. 375 ff., completed by the many studies made by the author, provides the
best source of information on the primitive hierarchy.

and at once two principles emerged from its conduct: First of all, the assembly, even for the liturgy, gathered round these 'witnesses'. It did not gather round a hierarchy of administrators as in the synagogue, nor of those who offered sacrifices as in the Temple, but round a missionary hierarchy of those who had been sent. An understanding of this relationship between mission and liturgy, witnessing and assembly, was to come later. It is important to emphasise that it existed from the beginning of the assembly and those who presided were responsible for the relations of the Church and the world.

Secondly, this presidency was collegial. The whole apostolic body directed the Jerusalem assembly. Peter presided. He spoke in the name of all (Acts 2:14–15; 37–38; 3:12–15), but always from within a collegiality.

Unfortunately, besides this group of apostles whose role was new and determinative, an institution, Jewish in type, continued the former Jewish structures in the Christian assembly. To understand the coexistence of the two different hierarchies, we should recall that the first Christians of Jerusalem, especially the Hebrews, were drawn from the best Jewish circles; particularly from the Pharisees who were so vehemently attached to the integrity of faith and Jewish practices, since they were convinced that Christianity was its fulfilment (Acts 21:20). In this light we can better understand the group of elders (*presbuteroi*) who correspond to the groups who had no specific sacrificial functions in Jewish assemblies. It seems likely that the apostles achieved a *modus vivendi* with this group, and often included them in their doctrinal decisions, ignoring certain actions which were incompatible with a real Christian spirit. This explains how Paul and Barnabas were introduced to the apostles and to the elders so that they could discuss together the ritual obligations that were to be imposed on Christians coming from paganism:

> And when Paul and Barnabas had no small dissension and debate with them, Paul and Barnabas and some of the others were appointed to go up to Jerusalem to the apostles and the elders about this question (Acts 15:2).

Elders and apostles also agreed to sign the letter that put an end to the questions raised at what has been called the 'council of Jerusalem':

> The brethren, both the apostles and the elders, to the brethren who are of the Gentiles in Antioch and Syria and Cilicia, greeting . . . (Acts 15:23).

The elders even controlled the purely missionary decisions of the apostles (Acts 11) and at times they acted alone (Acts 11:30).

James, the brother of the Lord, dominated this band of elders. Hebrew converts to Christianity were convinced that the prophecies about the assembly of the nations would be fulfilled in the presence of the descendant of David (Acts 1:6–7). So they instinctively turned to the Messiah's brothers who represented the line of David, as if the new people were to be directed by a dynastic hierarchy 'according to flesh and blood' and not 'according to the spirit' (Acts 1:13–14). Disturbed by the absence of Christ whom they had failed to 'recognise' in the signs of his presence (sacraments, apostolic powers, and so on) (John 20–21), they attempted to find him again in flesh and blood according to the hopes of Jewish messianism. It seems that this mentality prevailed for a long time in Jerusalem because James was replaced as head of the community by Simeon, another of Christ's brothers. Simeon in his turn was replaced by the son of Jude, a third brother of the Lord.[1]

When Paul went up to Jerusalem to greet Peter between 34 and 39, he found that he was also obliged to meet James, so decisive was the latter's influence:

> Then after three years I went up to Jerusalem to visit Cephas, and remained with him fifteen days. But I saw none of the other apostles except James the Lord's brother (Gal 1:18–19).

And if Paul succeeded in convincing Peter that the assembly of the nations was missionary in character (Acts 15:7–12), Peter's fine profession of faith was adroitly corrected by James and the elders who were sufficiently powerful to impose a more or less restrictive decree (Acts 15:13–21). On another occasion James was to extend the hand of fellowship to Paul (Gal 2:9) in

---

[1] Eusebius, *Ecclesiastical History*, III, 12, 19, 20.

recognition of the apostle's missionary work among the pagans, but also to make very clear that he was not to intervene in that portion of the flock that had come from Judaism and over which he himself intended to preserve all his own rights. He went so far as to send spies to see whether Paul's apostolic activity was confined to the pagan world.

> But because of false brethren secretly brought in, who slipped in to spy out our freedom which we have in Christ Jesus, that they might bring us into bondage – to them we did not yield submission even for a moment, that the truth of the gospel might be preserved for you (Gal 2:4–5).

This spying was to have consequences. Peter had to face 'certain persons who came from James' (Gal 2:12), and Paul was officially accused before James and the Jerusalem elders:

> You see, brother, how many thousands there are among the Jews of those who have believed; they have been told about you that you teach all the Jews who are among the Gentiles to forsake Moses (Acts 21:20–21).[1]

Such a situation necessarily led to the separation of the two jurisdictions:

> . . . we should go to the Gentiles and they to the circumcised (Gal. 2:9).

As if there were two ways of living the Christian faith! As if there were two communities within the household of the faith: the community of the strong and of the weak!

And so two hierarchies shared the direction of the Jerusalem assembly. It seems that the apostolic college was recognised for what it was, but it is equally certain that its action was checked and its influence thwarted by the elders and the brethren of Jesus.

The apostolic college based its claims on the gift of the Spirit and the missionary mandate received from the Lord. The college of elders relied on 'flesh and blood' and fidelity to Pharisaic tradition. The former was fundamentally open to the world even

---

[1] For more details see J. Dupont, *Pierre et Paul a Antioche et a Jerusalem*, Rc. Sc. Rel. 1957, pp. 42–60; 225–239.

if it had not yet made perfectly explicit this constitutive openness. The latter is completely closed in upon itself, bound by Jewish customs, exclusively concentrated on a messianic and dynastic conception of the future Kingdom. The first hierarchy is essentially missionary, the second administrative.

The drama of the Jerusalem assembly is the same as that of all the assemblies in the history of the Church. Would it gather round the apostolic college, making a missionary relation between the Church and the world the reason for every meeting as a Christian assembly? Or, on the contrary, would it gather round a hierarchy of elders, good administrators, concerned about their flock's zeal and virtue, more devoted to pastoral duties than to missionary concern?

In the twentieth century the attitude of James and the elders represents that of those parish priests, certainly concerned to sustain the virtues of practising Christians, but hardly inclined to encourage them to welcome the non-practising world. This attitude is still found among some of the native clergy in mission lands who assume care of the parishes and leave the work of evangelisation to foreign missionaries; as if it were possible to separate the mission from the community which established it, and as if the duties of the Christian assembly could be divided up into different fields of specialisation: on one hand those concerned with the care of souls, on the other, those concerned with the mission.

This was one of the causes of the religious decline in France in recent centuries when the parish clergy confined themselves to preserving the religious practice of their flocks, leaving to certain religious orders that had specialised in this field all the mission work. As if it were possible to separate this from the eucharistic assembly. This attitude may still be found in some centres of pastoral liturgy which concentrate on problems of rubrics and have little interest in collaborating with missionary institutions, as if it were possible to conceive a liturgical renewal not inspired by missionary concern.

How many pastors are more 'the brothers of the Lord' rather than real representatives of the 'apostles'? This was no doubt the examination of conscience made by the primitive Church when thinking of the Jerusalem crisis. The evangelists give us some hint of this when they relate with a certain complacency Christ's diatribes against the Pharisees (Matt 5:17; 23:13–36) and his severe judgement about his brothers:

> While he was still speaking to the people, behold, his mother and his brethren stood outside, asking to speak to him. But he replied to the man who told him, 'Who is my mother, and who are my brethren?' And stretching out his hand towards his disciples, he said, 'Here are my mother and my brethren! For whoever does the will of my Father in heaven is my brother, and sister, and mother' (Mt 12:46–50; cf. Lk 11:27–28; Jn 7:2–4).

Mark puts even greater emphasis on this judgement of the Lord when he contrasts the brothers of Jesus with the apostles (Mk 3:13–19, and 3:20–35).

How did Peter react to this situation?

If it is difficult to follow the stages of his thought, it is nevertheless possible to discern certain attitudes and clear signs that he was well aware of being the universal 'assembler' and that in this he differed from James and the elders. At first he continued to go to the Temple regularly (Acts 3:1, 19–26), but subsequently he seemed to keep his distance from the Hebrews. When he decided to leave Jerusalem (Easter 44, as if in fulfilment of the liberation which is contained in this feast), he sent a message to James stating this fact without taking the trouble to meet him personally:

> 'Tell this to James and to the brethren.' Then he departed and went to another place (Acts 12:17).

As long as he remained in the city, Peter was able to show that his primacy was of a different order from James's. He inspected some of the communities outside Jerusalem: Samaria (Acts 8:14), Caesarea (Acts 9:31–10:48); this was something no other member of the presbyterates grouped around the brother of the Lord had ever done. If at times he allowed himself to be so overinfluenced by Judaism as to accept for a moment the title of the Apostle of the Circumcised, he refused to be bound like James to a territory or a race. He became conscious of his role as an assembler, despite the weakness of his character which caused him to allow impossible compromises for which Paul did not hesitate to tax him with 'dissimulation'.

> But when Cephas came to Antioch I opposed him to his face, because he stood condemned. For before certain men came from James, he ate with the Gentiles; but when they came he drew back and separated himself, fearing the circumcision party. And with him the rest of the Jews acted insincerely, so that even Barnabas was carried away by their insincerity. But when I saw that they were not straightforward about the truth of the gospel, I said to Cephas before them all, 'If you, though a Jew, live like a Gentile and not like a Jew, how can you compel the Gentiles to live like Jews?' (Gal 2:11-14).

Peter, therefore, was obliged to leave Jerusalem to free himself from the sectarian plans made by James and the brothers of Jesus. And so we follow him to Antioch, then to Rome, and see all that he does to free the apostolic work of the assembly from all that might hamper it.

This analysis of the means employed by the Jerusalem community to bring men together teaches us the essential lesson that an assembly can call all nations together only if it is gathered around those who have received a mandate from the Lord. To the extent that an assembly sees its president as a minister of worship, or one who offers sacrifice, rather than a missionary, the essential meaning of the assembly – a sign of a universal gathering – is impaired. To realise his mission, Peter had to leave Jerusalem. Ought not many priests also to leave in spirit parish assemblies where they are regarded as purveyors of religious necessities rather than representatives and signs of the great assembly which is at work on a world-wide scale?

A COUNTERSIGN OF CATHOLICITY

At Pentecost, the memory of the assembly of tribes at Sinai, the presence of a very mixed crowd, the curious phenomenon of the gift of tongues that seized the apostles, the striking contrast between this assembly and the dispersion at Babel (Gen 11:1-9) – all this must have made these men aware that the 'catholic age' was beginning.

In asking the apostles to baptise them the Jews probably did not feel that they were changing their religion. In other words, the Judaeo-Christians considered the universal assembly to be essentially centripetal. This meant that in fulfilment of the prophecies the nations must come to honour the true God in Jerusalem and in so doing they would, as it were, make reparations for all the wrongs they had done to Israel during the centuries. Neither the Jews, nor the Judaeo-Christians, ever considered modifying their belief or their ritual to enable all nations to meet in a common faith and to take part in the same liturgy. They were prepared to think in universal terms, on condition that all nations were ready to accept one culture and one law: the Jewish culture and the Mosaic law.

Why blame the Hebrews for this? Is this attitude unknown today? Are there not Christians who rejoice at the thought of the conversion of others but who fail to realise that this conversion can only occur if Catholics themselves are converted radically and reform their ways? Many Christians pray for the missions and happily find in missionary progress a visible manifestation of the work of unification that God is achieving in the new churches of Africa and Asia; that is, they rejoice in the introduction of Western thought-patterns, the Latin language and European rites and ceremonies. Certain middle-class Christians congratulaty themselves because the Church is active among workers but thee may never stop to realise that if a worker today becomes a Christian he must not only accept Christianity in matters of faith and morals, but he must also accept a bourgeois culture and attitudes that are, in many ways, alien to him, and which Christ does not require of him.

This was precisely the attitude of the primitive Jerusalem community. They could exult over the conversion of the pagans:

> . . . they glorified God, saying, 'Then to the Gentiles also God has granted repentance unto life' (Acts 11:18; cf. 21:20),

but at the same time they imposed on them a Judaic way of life.

The consequences were disastrous. The Jerusalem assembly split into two communities composed of the strong and the weak, and what was meant to be a sign of unity was not far from schism.

Apostolic collegiality was impaired when Peter reserved power over the circumcised for himself and Paul was given charge over the uncircumcised (Gal 2:7), when according to divine institution the apostolic college is responsible for the whole mission for the whole human race.[1]

This division was also introduced with the community's charitable efforts. The elders assisted the needy and the widows who had been converted from Judaism, while the 'Seven' were responsible for Christians of the diaspora and hellenistic circles.[2]

> Now in these days when the disciples were increasing in number, the Hellenists murmured against the Hebrews because their widows were neglected in the daily distribution. And the twelve summoned the body of the disciples and said, 'It is not right that we should give up preaching the word of God to serve tables. Therefore, brethren, pick out from among you seven men of good repute, full of the Spirit and of wisdom, whom we may appoint to this duty. But we will devote ourselves to prayer and to the ministry of the word.' And what they said pleased the whole multitude, and they chose Stephen, a man full of faith and of the Holy Spirit, and Philip, and Prochorus, and Nicanor, and Timon, and Parmenas, and Nicolaus, a proselyte of Antioch. These they sat before the apostles, and they prayed and laid their hands upon them (Acts 6:1–6).

The college of the 'Seven' (sometimes wrongly given the title of deacons) was composed of men whose names have a Greek sound, did not limit themselves to the serving of tables. Nor did the Hebrew college of elders devote all their time to questions of government. The Seven at once made their influence felt by acting as 'assemblers' of the Hellenists. Stephen vigorously attacked the law, and like Christ, was martyred because of his attitude to the Temple:

> And they set up false witnesses who said, 'This man never ceases to speak words against this holy place and the law; for we have heard

---

[1] Yet Peter never observed this division of work which was far from catholic. As soon as pagans were converted, he hastened to assume full responsibility (Acts 8:14; 9:32; 10). So frequently did he visit communities comprised of former pagans that he was given the title of 'he who passes everywhere' (Acts 9:32), a perfect title for one who is aware of his duty as 'an assembler'.
[2] Cf. Delorme, *Les Hellenistes des actes des apôtres*, Ami du Clergé 1961, pp. 445–447.

him say that this Jesus of Nazareth will destroy this place, and will change the customs which Moses delivered to us' (Acts 6:13–14).

Philip hastened to make converts in Samaria, a region which orthodox Jews considered lost (John 4:9). There he converted many (Acts 8:4–8), and even went so far as to baptise a eunuch – a man excluded from religious assemblies by Jewish law – without even observing the usual stages of the catechumenate prescribed by Judaism for the baptism of proselytes (Acts 8:26–38). Philip's curious 'disappearance' (Acts 8:39) and his removal to Azotus by the Holy Spirit (Acts 8:40) might easily be connected with some condemnatory measure promulgated by the Jerusalem elders against this troublesome propagandist.

It may be exaggerated to say that the tension existing between Hebrews and Hellenists within the Jerusalem assembly went so far as the betrayal of the latter by the former.[1] Yet one point is certain, when the Jews persecuted the Christians, the victims were usually the converts from the diaspora.

Perhaps this is why men turned to Christ's teaching in order to find a solution of the problems. When Matthew joined the two narratives, separated in other traditions, of the cure of a leper and the son of the centurion (Mt 8:1–13), his purpose was obviously to make a contrast between the conduct of a Jew whose cure had to be legally certified and that of a pagan who, by faith alone, could obtain a more perfect result.

Luke contrasts the behaviour of nine Jewish lepers who were cured but who were also bound to observe the law with that of a Samaritan who, not bound by the law, was able to believe and to give thanks more perfectly than his companions (Lk 17:11–19). In this same perspective of hostility between the Hebrew and the Hellenistic communities, we should consider the parable of the workers in the vineyard in which those who were called during the first hour were invited not to be scandalised when those called later enjoyed the same access to the vineyard and God's grace (Mt 20:1–15). The parable of the prodigal is to be seen in the

[1] It should be made quite clear that when we call one of the Jerusalem communities the Hellenists, we do not imply that its recruitment was limited to Jews from the diaspora. Perhaps some of its members had been connected with the Qumrân movement.

same light. The elder son, watching jealously preparations being made for a banquet in honour of his younger brother, expressed the thought of Hebrews and Pharisees:

> Lo, these many years I have served you, and never disobeyed your command . . . (Lk 15:29).

The same lesson is found in the parables of the two sons (Mt 21:28–32) and the murderous wine dressers (Mt 21:33–44) which Matthew obviously revised with reference to the crisis which divided the communities between Hebrews and Hellenists.

Shortly after the composition of Matthew's Aramaic gospel, Paul, who had suffered because of the disapproval of the Jerusalem elders and who had found in all the communities that he established false brethren inviting the Christians to return to Judaism, proclaimed the absolute necessity of an assembly in which Jews and Gentiles would become one:

> For there is no distinction between Jew and Gentile; the same Lord is Lord of all and bestows his riches upon all who call upon him (Rom 10:12; cf. 1 Cor 12:13; Gal 3:28).

> Here there cannot be Greek and Jew, circumcised and uncircumcised, barbarian, Scythian, slave, freeman, but Christ is all, and in all (Col 3:11).

Unfortunately, the Jerusalem Christians did not understand such a message. Would it be better understood by modern assemblies?

THE FLIGHT FROM JERUSALEM AND THE FALL OF THE CITY

In 37 the Jewish authorities unleashed a violent persecution against the Christians of Jerusalem:

> And on that day a great persecution arose against the church (assembly) in Jerusalem; and they were all scattered throughout the region of Judea and Samaria . . . (Acts 8:1).

The Hellenists were the favourite victims: Stephen was the first (Acts 7:55–8:3). Six months later James, the apostle, was killed (Acts 12:1–5). Hebrew and Hellenist disciples fled from the city to escape persecution and established Christian communities in neighbouring parts of Judaea and Samaria. Philip, one of the Seven, returned to Samaria (Acts 8:4–8). Saul, the former persecutor, went to Damascus (Acts 9:19–25). Barnabas, a Levite, who had been particularly loyal to the Jerusalem community to which he had given all his goods (Acts 4:36–37), went to Antioch (Acts 11:22) where he was met by John Mark (Acts 12:25). But what results could be expected from evangelising activity being carried on by such scattered witnesses?

> Now those who were scattered because of the persecution that arose over Stephen travelled as far as Phoenicia and Cyprus and Antioch, speaking the word to none except Jews. But there were some of them, men of Cyprus and Cyrene, who on coming to Antioch spoke to the Greeks (Acts 11:19–20).

Reflecting on this flight of Christians from Jerusalem, the evangelists recalled Christ's teaching:

> Then let those who are in Judea flee to the mountains; let him who is on the housetop not go down to take what is in his house; and let him who is in the field not turn back to take his mantle . . . Pray that your flight may not be in winter or on a sabbath (Mt 24:16–20).

They saw this new experience as a repetition of the flight from Babylon (Isa 48:20; Jer 50:8; 51:6, 45; Apoc 18:4) which marked the beginning of the new people. In like manner the flight from Jerusalem would enable a new Remnant to be established, a new people. In fact, the fall of Jerusalem would be considered one of the great events in the history of religion, through which the Son of Man would be seen in the heavens and the nations would be gathered together:

> . . . so will be the coming of the Son of Man . . . then will appear the sign of the Son of Man in heaven, and then all the tribes of the earth will mourn, and they will see the Son of Man coming on the clouds of heaven with power and great glory; and he will send out his angels . . . and they will gather his elect from the four winds . . . (Mt 24:27, 30–31).

> . . . you will see the Son of Man seated at the right hand of Power and coming on the clouds of heaven (Mt 26:64).

It would take too long to show that these passages deal not only with the end of the world, but when they were written they referred to the coming fall of Jerusalem, a decisive event in primitive Christianity which was to free the apostles for ever from the equivocal situation which was fostered by James and the other elders. This event made possible the spread of the Church into Palestine and then into the whole world. It permitted the formulation of a spiritual religion open to all nations, without temple, without sacrificial worship, without legalism. At this moment the Son of Man did indeed begin his work of gathering together, and the men of all nations could 'beat their breast' in acknowledgement of his dominion and in response to his 'messengers' (or angels) sent throughout the world to proclaim his kingship.

The Jerusalem assembly formed an obstacle to this expansion. Not until the Christians had fled from Zion's walls and the city itself had been destroyed did circumstances and the Spirit enable the Church to think independently of Judaism and thus realise its universal mission.

THE ANTIOCH ASSEMBLY

. . . and in Antioch the disciples were for the first time called Christians (Acts 11:26).

Jerusalem Christians were so deeply involved in Judaism that they could think of themselves only as a sect among Jewish sects. Antioch Christians, on the contrary, were free and quickly became aware of their own individuality and originality.

THE FIGURE OF BARNABAS

Barnabas is the central figure in the Antioch assembly. Not that he was actually its founder, but he was its great inspiration and for this reason became one of the greatest apostles of the Church.

Barnabas, whose true Jewish name was Joseph, was born in Cyprus in the diaspora (Acts 4:26), but he lived in Jerusalem and served as a Levite in the Temple. This means that he had a detailed knowledge of Jewish worship and understood the liturgical doctrine of the Chosen People.

Converted by the preaching of the apostles, he became one of the first members of the Jerusalem community. He was a rich man, so he sold his property to become poor and so have the right to take part in the assembly of the poor gathered in Jerusalem.

> . . . sold a field which belonged to him, and brought the money and laid it at the apostles' feet (Acts 4:37).

His conversion should be placed between the years 30 and 35. No further details are given about him at this time except the fact that the apostles called him Barnabas (Acts 4:36). We do not exactly know why they gave him this name but it was amply justified during his later apostolate. Barnabas means 'son of encouragement' and this is precisely what he was, for he was able to unite Hebrews and Hellenists, assuming in his own person the conflicts and tensions of their division.

About the year 40, word reached Jerusalem that Saul, the persecutor, had been converted, that he had been active in Damascus and Arabia (Gal 1:17–18), and that he intended to come to Jerusalem. In other words, without any mandate from the mother community, Paul had made himself an apostle; he had proclaimed the Good News in pagan lands and now intended to appear in Jerusalem. How would this withdrawn community welcome this intruder?

> And when he had come to Jerusalem he attempted to join the disciples; and they were all afraid of him, for they did not believe that he was a disciple (Acts 9:26).

Barnabas had the courage to bring Paul to the assembly and introduce him to the apostles, thus establishing contact between the community and the stranger:

> But Barnabas took him, and brought him to the apostles and declared to them how on the road he had seen the Lord, who spoke to him, and how at Damascus he had preached boldly in the name of Jesus (Acts 9:27–28).

This was a beginning. A few years later, about 43, rumour reached Jerusalem that Christians from Cyprus and Cyrene had founded a community open to pagans in Antioch:

> . . . coming to Antioch, spoke to the Greeks, also, preaching the

Lord Jesus. And the hand of the Lord was with them, and a great number that believed turned to the Lord (Acts 11:20–21).

At once the Jerusalem community dispatched an inspector, as it had already sent Peter to see what Philip was doing (Acts 8:14). Barnabas was chosen for this mission which was in a certain sense apostolic (Acts 11:22). Barnabas reached Antioch and discovered the extent of the work accomplished by the Spirit. He decided to remain in the assembly:

When he came and saw the grace of God he was glad; and he exhorted them all to remain faithful to the Lord with steadfast purpose; for he was a good man, full of the Holy Spirit and of faith. And a large company was added to the Lord. So Barnabas went to Tarsus to look for Saul; and when he had found him, he brought him to Antioch. For a whole year they met with the church (assembly) and taught a large company of people . . . (Acts 11:23–26).

While Peter remained involved in the particularism of the Jerusalem community, Barnabas was discovering the true dimensions of the role of 'assembler' that had been given to the apostles. Peter scarcely dared to risk the evangelisation of Judaea and Samaria, and felt obliged to defend himself when he baptised a pagan in Caesarea; Barnabas, on the other hand, considered himself free to preach to the whole world. With Paul, he visited Cyprus, Pisidia, Iconium, Lycaonia, Lystra and many other Greek towns (Acts 13–14). Peter had to use all his power to close the widening breach that was developing between Hebrews and Hellenists; Barnabas encouraged his community in a charitable project on behalf of the Jerusalem poor without any thought of racial divisions (Acts 11:27–30).

Perhaps it was his desire to be all things to all men, to Jews as to Greeks, that inspired him to be more Jewish than was necessary (Gal 2:13). It is not unlikely that Barnabas was responsible for the letter to the Hebrews which was precisely for those Jews who had fled from Jerusalem under threat of persecution, and in exile regretted the loss of the Temple with all its liturgical assemblies. They also disdained the charity of the Christian assembly, a spiritual temple which would have given them a true priesthood.

A NEW KIND OF HIERARCHY

At the beginning, the Christian community of Antioch grouped the Jerusalem exiles with the Jews and the pagans. Perhaps it already had its 'prophets' and 'doctors' (as in Acts 11:27 and 13:1), but the establishment of Christians in their city must have followed the same pattern as the establishment of Jews in the big cities at this time. Small local communities, each with its own structure and duties, only met together rarely.

At this stage of its development, the Antioch community had opened its doors to pagans; nevertheless it remained basically Jewish. Barnabas arrived. At once he defined the role of the assembly. This was a new role unknown to the ancient Jewish hierarchies. All the little local communities should meet together in faith and love:

> He encouraged them to continue steadfast in heart and faithful to the Lord (Acts 11:23).[1]

The people became an assembly with the arrival of Barnabas the apostle (Acts 11:24):

> ... For a whole year they met with the church, and taught a large company of people ... (Acts 11:26).

Barnabas did not appear in Antioch as the supreme head of an already established organisation nor as one who offers sacrifice, but essentially as a missionary proclaiming the Word to the world and consequently having the right to preside over the assembly. After a year of ministry, Barnabas and Saul were given a more general missionary vocation.

> While they were worshipping the Lord and fasting, the Holy Spirit said, 'Set apart for me Barnabas and Saul for the work to which I have called them.' Then after fasting and praying they laid their hands on them and sent them off (Acts 13:2-3).[2]

This ceremony was not an episcopal consecration. Such an idea would be a strange anachronism. Nor is it a rite giving two of its

[1] This translation follows a textual variant.
[2] See Peterson, *La 'leitourgia' des prophètes et des didascales à Antioche*, Re. Sc. Rel. 1949, pp. 576-579.

members a missionary and apostolic character. Both Barnabas and Saul were apostles before they reached Antioch. Actually it was agreed by the liturgical assembly that they should have at their head apostles whose function it was to call all men into one assembly. Had the Antioch Christians retained these apostles in their midst, they would have reduced these two men to the rank of simple offerers of sacrifice, doctors or local chiefs. This would be to limit the Christian hierarchy whose function it is to transcend local situations, to express the desire for universalism and to be an ever-present reminder to the communities which they control of the importance of a universal fellowship.

Antioch sent Paul and Barnabas on a mission but no effort was made to replace them at home because present or absent, they continued to be the centre of the assembly and, through their spoken or written word, reminded the community of their role as a universal assembly. Antioch functioned on the local level through the efforts of its elders, prophets, and doctors but its true centre was always the apostle, even when he was far away from his community.

The relevance of all this for today's world is plain. How many of today's liturgical assemblies realise that the most important element is not to be found in the priests who supply their religious needs, adminster the sacraments and organise the life of the Christians, but that it is to be found in the relation of the community with the missionary who is charged with the fulfilment of God's universalist plan and the communication of this truth to the assembly over which he presides? Paul made this clear to the Corinthians: 'Christ did not send me to you to baptise but to proclaim the Gospel' (1 Cor 1:17).

The relation of our parish communities to the bishop should be re-examined in the light of the Antioch experience. This would lead to important changes in the lives of the local assemblies and of the bishops.

Antioch selected the members of its hierarchy because of their role in the ministry of the Word. First, there was the apostle whose word summoned men. Then came the prophets who announced or interpreted the Word of God in the assemblies. Lastly, there are the doctors who gave the brethren doctrinal and moral teaching (Acts 13:1). St Paul later pointed out the reasons for the establishment of this hierarchy (1 Cor 12–14); it is necessary to note here that its existence depends more than anything else on the Word.

It is difficult to decide whether there was a group of elders in Antioch corresponding to the group in Jerusalem. Acts does not allude to them. Yet every town visited at this time by Paul and Barnabas (Lystra, Iconium, Antioch, Pisidia) possessed such a body. It seems most likely that the two apostles also established one at Antioch. But the spirit in which they operated was utterly different. The Jerusalem group was all-powerful. Its members were elected by the community just as in the communities of the diaspora. Paul and Barnabas, on the contrary, appointed the college of elders in the communities that they founded.

And when they had appointed elders for them in every church (assembly), with prayer and fasting, they committed them to the Lord in whom they believed (Acts 14:23).

The elders were subject to the apostle. They were not an independent group able to impede the general activities of the apostles as they were in Jerusalem. They were not an autonomous group as in the Jewish communities. They were placed directly under the apostle's jurisdiction so that, like him, they became a means of assembly. The local community could never limit itself to its own interests. Its leaders were inspired by the great universalist spirit of the apostles.

At Antioch, then, with the presence of the apostles, the organisation of the hierarchy centred on the charism of the Word, and probably the help of a group of elders, the hierarchy was constituted and adapted to its essential mission which was to call men into communities, which were the authentic signs of assembly.

THE COLLECTION FOR JERUSALEM

While the Jerusalem community was divided into small groups for the distribution of charity to its own members (Acts 6:1–6), Antioch prepared an 'ecumenical' collection. This step had an important effect in the primitive Church. Far more than a single philanthropic project, it was a new sign of assembly and universalism.

During the year 48, there was a severe famine in Judaea and Jerusalem, aggravated by the fact that the preceding year had been a jubilee year and there had been hardly any harvest. Many sent help. Jewish sources recall the gifts of Queen Adiabene. But the efforts of the Antioch Christians were inspired by the Holy Spirit, the Spirit of unity and union:

> And one of them (prophets) named Agabus stood up and foretold by the Spirit that there would be a great famine over all the world; and this took place in the days of Claudius. And the disciples determined, every one according to his ability, to send relief to the brethren who lived in Judea; and they did so, sending it to the elders by the hand of Barnabas and Saul (Acts 11:28–30).

The Antioch community was careful to entrust its gift to Paul and Barnabas, the representatives of catholicity and universality. The act of charity thus became a sign of the union of the two communities, a sign of the assembly of all men in God's love.

One of the principal arguments Paul advanced in favour of this collection was precisely the *koinōnia* it would establish between the assemblies:

> ... you (the Christians of Jerusalem) will glorify God ... by the generosity of your contribution for them and for all others ... (2 Cor 9:13; cf. Rom 15:26–27; 2 Cor 8:4).

Perhaps, when collecting 'the treasures of the nations' to bring them to Jerusalem, Paul recalled the prophecy of Isaiah (60:9; cf. Rom 15:26–27). His vocabulary suggests this:

> For the coastlands shall wait for me,
>   the ships of Tarshish first,
> to bring your sons from afar,
>   their silver and gold with them ...
>
> you shall suck the breast of kings
> and you shall know that I, the Lord,
>   am your Saviour (Isa 60:9, 16).

In any case, he took care that the collection should be an act of the Sunday assembly, and not merely the sum of individual charitable efforts:

> On the first day of every week, each of you is to put aside something and store it up . . . (1 Cor 16:2).

St Paul wrote these directives in the years immediately after the initiative taken by the Antioch community. That is, his doctrine is the result of his experience. Once again this community fully fulfilled its role as the typical Christian assembly. It expressed its desire to emerge from its own boundaries, and its refusal to be a community turned in upon itself; it was concerned, on the contrary, to be a sign of that universal assembly progressively effected by the Lord.

THE SUNDAY ASSEMBLY

This investigation of the Antioch community suggests a study of the spirit of the Sunday assembly, a sign of the universal assembly to which the Antiochenes aspired. Hypotheses of many scholars point to the conclusion that the city of Antioch was the place where both Matthew's gospel and the 'Teaching of the Twelve Apostles' (the *Didache*) were composed.[1] This work was probably begun in the first century and the first draft of the *Didache* must have been prepared while the Matthean traditions were being recorded. In other words in the *Didache* we have abundant information about the Antioch community shortly after its establishment.

[1] See for Matthew, G. D. Kilpatrick, *The Origins of the Gospel according to St Matthew*, Oxford 1946, p. 130; B. Gerhardsson, *Matteusevangelist och Judekristendomen*, S.E.A. 1959, pp. 97–100. For the *Didache*, see: J. P. Audet, *Les instructions des apôtres*, 1958, pp. 206 ff. These are hypotheses. Yet the evidence on certain points approaches *quasi certitude*. For example, the close relation between the *Didache* and the Matthean traditions, the impossibility of separating these two works, the *quasi certitude* that they spring from a community well aware of the problem of the Gentile missions and the problems of the second half of the first century in Palestine and in Syria. If exegetes indicate a preference for Antioch, it is because this church is the only church about which there is sufficient information and where was best realised a form of the perfect assembly as opposed to the Jerusalem assembly. In any case, it is probably true that Matthew and the *Didache* were written in a community which, like Antioch, was the result of the same emigration from Jerusalem and which faced the same problems.

We can adopt here the following reconstruction of the celebration of vigils at Antioch, as suggested by J. P. Audet.[1]

First of all we learn of the ritual. Essentially the vigils were made up of the 'breaking of bread', according to the Jewish custom, followed by the great 'eucharist', properly so called. Between these two celebrations there was a short rite of transition with a procession from one place to another. Here are some of the details.

The first part was open to Christians and sympathetic pagans. Yet this welcom by the Christian community of the latter did not go as far as to allow them to take part in the actual eucharistic meal.

That no one eat nor drink of your 'eucharist' if he is not baptised in the name of the Lord. For concerning this also did the Lord say, 'Give not that which is holy to the dogs' (Did 9:5).

Everything in this first gathering recalled the Jewish breaking of bread. While a 'cup of blessing' and bread was being passed round in the assembly, the president blessed God for the wonders he had worked:

First concerning the Cup, 'We give thanks to you, our Father, for the Holy Vine of David your child, which you made known to us through Jesus your child' (Did 9:2).

The assembly answered: 'To you the glory for ever and ever. Amen' (Did 9:2). The president continued while breaking the bread:

We give you thanks, our Father, for the life and knowledge which you made known to us through Jesus your child (Did 9:3).

The assembly intervened again: 'To you the glory for ever and ever. Amen' (Did 9:3).

The celebrant continued:

As this broken bread was scattered upon the mountains, but was brought together and became one, so let your Church be gathered together from the ends of the earth into your kingdom (Did 9:4).

For the last time the assembly answered with its refrain:

[1] Op. cit., pp. 372-430.

For yours is the glory and the power through Jesus Christ for ever (Did 9:4).

Then they proceeded to the actual meal. When all were satisfied the president said the words:

We give thanks to you, Holy Father, for your Holy Name which you made to dwell in our hearts, and for the knowledge and faith and immortality which you made known to us through Jesus your Child (Did 10:2).

Once again the assembly chanted its refrain, then the president continued:

Lord Almighty, you created all things for your Name's sake and gave food and drink to men for their enjoyment that they might give you thanks, but you have blessed us with spiritual food and drink and eternal light through your Child. Above all we give thanks to you because you are mighty (Did 10:3-4).

The assembly intervened again, and the celebrant continued:

Remember, Lord, your Church, to deliver it from all evil and to make it perfect in your love, and gather it together in its holiness from the four winds to your kingdom which you have prepared for it (Did 10:5).

Then the meal ended with these words:

For to you belong the power and the glory for ever (Did 10:5).

Then perhaps they went to the place reserved for the great eucharist. The following dialogue there took place:

President: Let grace come and let this world pass away.

Assembly: Hosannah to the God of David.

President: If any man be holy, let him come! If any man be not, let him repent.

President: Maranatha!

Assembly: Amen (Did 10:6).

What inspired these communicants is therefore quite clear. A 'marvel' had taken place: Jesus Christ had appeared, and at once men had assembled together to bless the Father for sending his Son and to hope for the completion of his work, the gathering together in his Kingdom of men from the four corners of the world. The assembled community had no other concern than this 'gathering' of all the nations. They no longer believed that this would take place in Jerusalem but in the Kingdom prepared by the Son. Temple sacrifices were no longer prerequisites for this coming, but instead the 'knowledge' of God's plan, accomplished in Jesus and in the Church. Pagans were invited to this gathering and were encouraged to be converted (Did 10:6). The Church's missionary activity was the essential theme of the Antioch liturgical meeting.

The presence of pagans at such meetings is only possible, as has been said, when the way in which the worship is conducted is sufficiently spiritual to enable men of different cultures and races to assemble. That is why 'spiritual food and drink' (Did 10:4) replace bread and wine, and why the assembly of nations in the Kingdom of God is hailed rather than in the Temple of Zion, and why the shout 'hosanna to the house of David' – hitherto reserved to the Temple in Jerusalem – isused to express the assembly's awareness, at the eucharistic celebration, of being itself the new 'house of David' open to all mankind, and why finally it appeals to the 'knowledge' of faith which alone can unite different mentalities.

The Antioch assembly became aware that its own unity and its slow advance towards 'the perfection of love' (Did 10:5) as well as the great eucharist that the community celebrated at the close of its vigil, already constituted a sign of the final assembly. The president unhesitatingly pronounced the eschatological acclamation: Maranatha!, 'Come, Lord' at the very beginning of the eucharist. The Antioch assembly did become lost in a vague eschatologism. Both its charity and its eucharist are the concrete signs of the future assembly.

A few years later, the 'Teachings of the Apostles' received an addition in which we find a new view of the Sunday assembly at Antioch:

On the Lord's Day come together, break bread and hold Eucharist, after confessing your transgressions that your offering may be pure; but let none who has a quarrel with his fellow join in your meeting until they be reconciled, that your sacrifice be not defiled. For this is that which was spoken by the Lord, 'In every place and time offer me a pure sacrifice, for I am a great king,' says the Lord, 'and my name is wonderful among the heathen' (Did 14:1–3).

The assembly continues to be offered in two stages: the breaking of bread and the eucharist, but a new detail is provided, and for the first time we are told that this celebration takes place once a week, 'on the Lord's day'. And another idea is emphasised: the eucharist is a sacrifice. For this sacrifice to be pure, man should first confess his sins (cf. Mt 1:11); for the sacrifice to be offered without any fault, man should first reconcile himself with those whom he has offended (cf. Mt 5:23–24); for the sacrifice to be offered at all times and in all places, not only at certain times and in one temple, man should purify himself for the sacrifice to have a truly spiritual meaning. Antioch Christians need no longer envy those who live in Jerusalem. The Temple may now be destroyed. Those who live in Antioch can offer the true sacrifice that alone can unite all men, the spiritual sacrifice requiring no preparation of baths and purifications, but attitudes of charity, mutual forgiveness, and the confession of sins.

Whatever the date when this document was drawn up, it is of undeniable importance and forms a preparatory stage for the theology of the Epistle to the Hebrews.

When persecution broke up the Christian community in Jerusalem, many of its members sought refuge in Syria and Antioch.

Now those who were scattered because of the persecution that arose over Stephen travelled as far as Phoenicia and Cyprus and Antioch . . . (Acts 11:19).

These refugees, like all refugees, dreamt about the re-establishment of past situations and were fiercely intransigent in their fidelity to old traditions. They could think of nothing save their return to Jerusalem and taking part in Temple worship. They even considered abandoning the religion of Christ, who had separated them from Zion, so that they could embrace Judaism which would automatically give them access to the holy city.

To dispel these doubts, the Church, after considerable thought, produced the *Didache* and the letter to the Hebrews (probably composed at the same time as *Didache* 14), which the Christians of Antioch must have received on the same grounds as the other 'exiles' of this period. As in the *Didache*, the author of the letter to the Hebrews emphasises the role of the Sunday assembly as a sign of the eschatological assembly:

Having therefore, brethren, boldness to enter into the holiest by the blood of Jesus, by a new and living way, which he hath consecrated for us, through the curtain, that is, through his flesh, and since we have a great priest over the house of God, let us draw near with a true heart in full assurance of faith, with our hearts sprinkled clean from an evil conscience and our bodies washed with pure water. Let us hold fast the confession of our hopes without wavering, for he who promised is faithful; and let us consider how to stir up one another to love and good works, not neglecting to meet together, as is the habit of some, but encouraging one another, and all the more as you see the Day drawing near (Heb 10:19–25).

In this passage we find all the elements of the spiritual sacrifice enumerated in the *Didache*: confession of sins, mutual charity, eager expectation of the day of the assembly of mankind. All these were henceforth to replace the Temple sacrifices. Why should the Christian religion once again make the Jerusalem Temple its centre? This would be to choose a material city as a centre, whereas the Christian assembly is the meeting of the first-born of a heavenly city.

But you have come to Mount Zion and to the city of the living God, the heavenly Jerusalem, and to innumerable angels in festal gathering and to the assembly of the first-born who are enrolled in heaven, and to a judge who is God of all, and to the spirits of just men made perfect, and to Jesus, the mediator of a new covenant and to the sprinkled blood that speaks more graciously than the blood of Abel (Heb. 12:22–24).

This clarification of the theology of spiritual sacrifice justifies two important conclusions.

First of all, it will be recalled that this doctrine of spiritual sacrifice was formulated in a missionary context. This means that a rite had to be found which would gather all men together in one and the same hope, and this enabled the doctrine of spiritual sacrifice to be formulated. To lose sight of this spiritual concept can only mean that our eucharist and our assembly will become local and Judaic. Are not the least missionary-minded Christians those who are the most rigidly attached to narrow ritual forms such as the use of Latin or a particular civilisation? This suggests that true liturgical reform can be made only in a missionary climate, by those who are missionary-minded and well aware of the relation between the Church and the world.

The second conclusion to be drawn from the doctrine of spiritual sacrifice concerns the sacerdotal value of the Christian assembly. In the Jewish type of assembly, as it took place in the Temple, the sacrificial and sacerdotal power was vested in the high priest who, only after many purifications, was able to offer a sacrifice pleasing to God. The people were present at this sacrificial service but they were not sufficiently involved to merit being called a priestly people.

But since Christ fully and once for all took on the priestly and sacrificial function and instituted a new type of sacrifice of the spiritual order consisting essentially of love and obedience to the Father's plan (Heb 10:1–18), every man able to share these sentiments can unite himself with Christ's priesthood. Clearly the liturgical assembly of those who love each other in the Lord constitutes a true priestly people and a far more authentic temple than that of Zion. Peter was to say later:

Come to him, to that living stone, rejected by men but in God's sight chosen and precious; and like living stones be yourselves built into a spiritual house, to be a holy priesthood, to offer spiritual sacrifices acceptable to God through Jesus Christ. For it stands in scripture:

'Behold, I am laying in Zion a stone,
a cornerstone chosen and precious
and he who believes in him will not
be put to shame' (1 Pet 2:4–6; cf. 1 Pet 2:9).

Moreover, it is significant that in the whole of the New Testament the words 'priest' and 'offerer of sacrifice' are never attributed to men but only to Christ and to the Christian people. If there is a hierarchy within the assembly, it cannot be exclusively priestly and sacrificial. Its function will be to highlight the value of the assembly's priesthood by uniting it with Christ's priesthood.

This explains why at the heart of the Antioch assembly we find a hierarchy[1] essentially consecrated to the ministry of the Word (apostles, prophets, doctors) and to the service of the diaconate.[2] To be even more exact, it was at the moment when the writer of the latest part of the *Didache* defined the spiritual and missionary sacrifice of the Antioch community that he derived from this sacrifice, as a conclusion to his premises, the new type of Christian hierarchy:

> Appoint therefore for yourselves bishops and deacons worthy of the Lord, meek men, and not lovers of money, and truthful and approved, for they also minister to you the ministry of the prophets and teachers. Therefore do not despise them, for they are your honorable men together with the prophets and teachers (Did 15:1–2).

The assembly, therefore, was directed by those who brought the Word to it or who served it; those who, by the Word, unceasingly proclaimed the plan of God to it so that in a spirit of obedience those who served him could become a living assembly capable of exercising their spiritual priesthood in union with the priesthood of Christ. The bearer of the Word, an apostle or a prophet, was to preside over the assembly so that he who had preached the Good News or the Word of God would turn this preaching into thanksgiving and into 'eucharist':

> Allow the prophets to announce the blessing according to their good pleasure (Did 10:7).

AN ACCOUNT OF THE GATHERING EFFECTED
BY THE ANTIOCH ASSEMBLY

If Matthew's gospel was really composed in a Christian community like Antioch, we have some chance of discovering, in the themes peculiar to this evangelist, or in the way he arranged the

---

[1] Cf. p. 86.

[2] Here the diaconate is used in a wider sense than that of 'deacons'. Cf. *diakonia* in the sense of 'service' or 'minister' in Rom 12:7; 1 Cor 12:5; 16:15; 1 Cor 3:7–4:1; 8:4; etc., or in the more general sense of 'envoy' or of 'mission' as in Acts 11:29; 12:25; 20:24; 21:19; etc.

documents that he consulted, an echo of the special insights of the Antioch community.[1] More than any of the other evangelists, Matthew is concerned about the assembly and the conditions in which it may succeed or, on the contrary, run the risk of failure.

In the climate that prevailed at Antioch, and in the other Christian assemblies separated from the liturgy of Jerusalem, as they were obliged to think out their meetings for worship independently of the Temple sacrifices, a passage like Jeremiah 7 could not fail to hold their attention. Here the prophet condemned the worship offered in the Temple, which had been transformed into a 'den of thieves' (Jer 7:11): and foretold God's curse in the form of the withering of fruit trees (Jer 7:20); and proclaimed that God, who had never wanted any holocaust nor laid down anything at all about sacrifices (Jer 7:22), requires only obedience to his Word and to the Word of his prophets (Jer 7:25–28)!

No better text can be found in the Old Testament to justify the doctrine of spiritual sacrifice or the assembly gathered around the Word of the prophets and apostles, or a worship which was celebrated outside the Temple. Indeed, Christian midrashim were quickly composed to comment on this chapter of Jeremiah. This seems to be the origin of the tradition used by Matthew (21:12–45) which shows[2] how Christ, on the day of the purification of the Temple, sought to 'fulfil' the prophecy of Jeremiah; those seeking a new type of assembly would find in this tradition valuable food for thought.

Much more so than the other evangelists, Matthew respected this source and took pleasure in showing the Lord gathering one after the other in the Temple all the categories of people excluded from the Temple liturgy: the pagans, the lame, the blind, the children (Mt 21:12–16).[3] He deliberately placed the parable of the feast immediately after the midrashic tradition of Jeremiah 7

---

[1] If the hypothesis of an Antiochene edition of Matthew seems unlikely to our readers, they will have no difficulty in reading this paragraph as a conclusion to Chapter 2.

[2] See J. W. Doeve, *Purification du temple et desséchement du figuier*, N.T.S. 1954–1955, pp. 297–308. See the allusion to Jer 7:11 in Mt 21:13; to Jer 7:20 in Mt 21:18–19; to Jer 7:25–26 in Mt 21:23–37, and to Jer 7:27 in Mt 21:28–32.

[3] See the commentary in Chapter 2, p. 41.

(Mt 22:1–10), whereas Luke places it in another context (Lk 14:16–24). The contrast of the banquet hall with the temple court as the setting for the new assembly effectively points to the difference between the assembly to which the good and the bad were invited, and the temple service to which only the good and the 'clean' could come. There is also a dramatic touch. God summoned all men to the new assembly, and those who were invited persecuted those who were sent to them (Mt 22:6). This is an allusion to the persecution of the first Christians by their Jewish brothers. Traitors were lurking even within the groups of those who replied to the invitation (cf. the parable of the wedding garment, Mt 22:11–14).

Just as the story of the purification of the Temple was to persuade Christians that it was vital that the assembly should be open to everyone, the parable of the assembly in the banquet room was meant to convince the brethren in Antioch that the assembly in which they were to take part must be painful and must be held outside the Temple which was soon to be wiped off the map.

> The king was angry and he sent his troops and destroyed those murderers and burned their city (Mt 22:7).

If we compare Luke's version of the same parable of the banquet, we shall see that it is just as missionary- and assembly-minded, but that it is stripped of all drama (Lk 14:16–24). Matthew must have drawn up his account in a climate of thought similar to that which existed in Antioch where the best members still looked towards Jerusalem and were still only at the first stages of a theology of the Christian assembly which would free them from their temple complex.

Matthew offers us a diagnosis enabling us to discover the motives which, in his view, impelled some men to refuse the summons to the new assembly. Borrowing from old gospel traditions the account of the opposition between the Herodians, the Sadducees and the Pharisees (Mt 22:15–46), he inserted it immediately after the parable of the banquet (Luke places it in another context), and illustrates in this way the refusals mentioned in the parable. Those who will not accept the Lord's

invitation are those who belong to 'Caesar' rather than to the
Lord, or those who deny the existence of a Kingdom that is to
come, a Kingdom based on the resurrection, and above all those
who, like the Pharisees, trust in a legalistic religion. This description of the three typical attitudes of refusal of the invitation closes with a curse on all those who make these attitudes their
own, a curse in which we can discern the errors committed by the
Pharisees in their way of summoning men:

> . . . and they love the place of honour at feasts and the best seats in
> the synagogues . . . (Mt 23:6).

> But woe to you, scribes and Pharisees, hypocrites! because you shut
> the kingdom of heaven against men; for you neither enter yourselves,
> nor allow those who would enter to go in. Woe to you, scribes and
> Pharisees, hypocrites! for you traverse sea and land to make a single
> proselyte, and when he becomes a proselyte, you make him twice as
> much a child of hell as yourselves (Mt 23:13–15).

The final word on these curses is found in the Lord's condemnation of Jerusalem, a city which was meant to assemble and to be
assembled, but which was condemned for its obstinacy:

> Jerusalem, Jerusalem . . . How often would I have gathered your
> children together . . . (Mt 23:37).

Matthew was now ready to return to the common evangelical
tradition and transmit the Lord's eschatological discourse (Mt
24) in a new light: the destruction of Jerusalem in the near
future would create the perfect circumstances for the coming of
the Son of Man, and the assembly of all men round the Lord 'in
glory and in power' and not round the Temple.[1] In Chapter 25,
however, the evangelist felt free once more to describe the
people assembled by him who is to come. Just as there were three
categories of people opposed to the summons, the Sadducees,
the Herodians, and the Pharisees (Mt 22:15–45), we now see
three categories of people in favour of the summons: the servants,
in whom we can recognise the heads of communities (Mt 24:45–
51); the virgins (Mt 25:1–13); and the laymen (Mt 25:14–46).
Corresponding to the curses which those who opposed the

[1] See the commentary of this text in Chapter 2, p. 56.

assembly drew down upon themselves (Mt 23), we now see the blessings accorded those who are willing to be gathered together in the Kingdom.

Blessed is the servant whom his master when he comes will find so doing . . . (Mt 24:46).

Well done, good and faithful servant . . . enter into the joy of your master's (Mt 25:21).

Come, O blessed of my Father, inherit the kingdom prepared for you from the foundation of the world . . . (Mt 25:34).

Perhaps these chapters in Matthew (21–25) do not give us any new ideas about the assembly. Nevertheless, they show us how an evangelist wanted to respond to the problems raised in the Christian assembly and to bring to bear on them the light of the gospel tradition.

AFTER THE APOSTLES

Fifty years later the Antioch community had lost its apostles. How was the question of their succession solved in a city where there had been such insistence on the importance of having an apostle as the head?

It is rather surprising that although the sources of information are silent on the Church of the second century, there is abundant evidence on the life of the Antioch assembly at the beginning of this century. This community therefore plays an important role in the development of the theology of the assembly.

According to the correspondence of Ignatius it was the elders or the members of the *presbyterium* who directed the communities after the death of the apostles. This group of elders was guided by a bishop and this would seem to indicate that the old Jewish hierarchy, such as it conceived in the synagogues of the diaspora, was also imposed upon the Christian assemblies. Ignatius often alludes to this.

You should all honour the 'ministers' (*diakonoi*) as if they were Christ himself, the bishop as if he were the 'image' of the Father, the elders as if they were the senate of God and the college of the apostles. Without them, there would be no assembly (Trall, 3).

A return had apparently been made to a Jewish form of hierarchy, local in structure and therefore dangerously foreign to any missionary activity. But the climate of thought had changed. The college of elders, together with their bishop, was to become the sign of the inner unity of the assembly. Through its bishop, it was, above all, to become the sign of universality and mission to the world, thus avoiding all the dangers that 'localisation' might have entailed.

The bishop surrounded by his *presbyterium*, was always the sign of the internal unity of the assembly, especially during the schisms which already threatened the Church:

> Take care to participate in no more than one eucharist. There is in fact only one body of our Lord, only one cup which unites us in his blood, only one altar, just as there is only one bishop surrounded by the elders and the deacons, the associates of his service: thus you will fulfil God's will in all things (Philad 4).

One of the chief threats of schism came from Christians who wanted to return to Judaism, and to the old elements of the law and temple worship. Ignatius met this threat by recalling, in the best Antiochene tradition, that the eucharistic assembly where the bishops and elders presided constituted the new temple of the assembly:

> Remember that you are the stones of the Father's temple, stones that are meant to become part of the edifice constructed by God the Father, stones that are raised to the pinnacle through the instrument of Jesus Christ which is his cross and with the help of the Holy Spirit which is the cable. Your faith is the windlass, your charity is the way that leads to God. You are therefore bearing your God and his temple (Eph 9).

For this reason the Christian cannot absent himself from the assembly:

> Not to attend the assembly is an act of pride and an act of self-excommunication (Eph 5).

The bishop's only care must be to increase the number of assemblies:

> Therefore take care to hold frequent assemblies to offer God your

Eucharist and praise. Because when you come together often you crush Satan's power (Eph 13).

Hold assemblies more frequently. Summon the faithful to come to them (Polyc 4).

The local assembly, then, is the sign of unity and of gathering together. Outside the assembly there is only division and schism.

But the bishop of Antioch also knows that he must make his assembly live in harmony with the universal mission. The head of the community is no longer a wanderer. Yet if he is bound to one place, his constant care must be to move away, at least in spirit, and to be responsible for other assemblies. That is why Ignatius, Bishop of Antioch, wrote to six of them.

He chose a happy phrase to describe his care for all: 'I sing of the assemblies' (Magn 1) and he showed how the bishops who preside over each one live in collegiality:

Established as far as the ends of the earth,[1] the bishops are only one with the spirit of Jesus Christ (Eph 3).

The more they assemble, the more they seek new occasions for bringing their assemblies in contact with one another, the more they manifest this unity. Thus when Ignatius was travelling through Asia he met the other bishops.

My spirit, to greet you, is united with the charitable churches which received me in the name of Jesus Christ, not as a mere passerby because even those who were not on my route (I mean the route taken by my body) went to the nearest town and waited for me (Rom 9).

Ignatius took advantage of the end of persecution in his own city to suggest to the churches which he had met on his travels that they should send their bishop or their ministers to visit him.

As an assembly of God you should choose a minister (*diakonos*) and entrust to him the holy mission of bringing your congratulations to the Christians assembled in Antioch (Philad 10).

Here we should recall the charitable efforts made in Antioch to establish relations with the Jerusalem assembly. This is the

[1] It is then the theme of the universal mission which establishes the unity of the college of bishops.

purpose of the trip and the communication from assembly to assembly. And it is in the eucharistic assembly that this inter-communion is achieved.

As a consequence the bishop was now given two functions which did not belong to the elders of the Jerusalem Jewish community or of the Christian assembly. First of all, he was the president of the group of elders, soon to be called the *presbyterium*, the true shepherd of the local flock, the incarnation of a particular community. But at the same time he was the member of a college of bishops who wanted to live together and cause their communities to live in a climate of communion as a sign of the world-wide communion that God wished to achieve. The apostle who moved from one place to another in order to give a global dimension to his assembly was succeeded by a bishop who wished to achieve the same dimension by his life as a member of a college of bishops.

CONCLUSION

The members of the Antioch community were the first disciples to deserve the name of 'Christian'. In fact, for the first time a Christian assembly perfectly achieved the objectives laid down by the Lord. For the fifty years that we can follow the development of this assembly we can see that it always refused to allow itself to become merely 'local' or to concern itself exclusively with the religious problems of a social or geographical group. At one time, it was an apostle who gave it a missionary or universal dimension; at another, it was its bishop, living in collegiality with other bishops, who thus ensured the necessary ecumenical dimension of its assembly.

The worship of this assembly was no longer centred on the Temple or on those who offered the sacrifice of the former liturgies. The community itself was the temple where the new ministers 'serve', making possible the spiritual sacrifice of each one, in love and obedience, according to the divine plan. On the basis of this idea the assembly could offer to pagans and to Jews a form of worship at which all could be present without experiencing the exclusiveness of any one culture or people. And it was through the same idea, also, that gradually the assembly became aware of its priestly character and the entirely new function of its leaders. As ministers of the Word, they encouraged the faithful to those attitudes of soul that constitute a spiritual sacrifice; in their role as servants of a community which they formed and organised, they helped others to participate in the Lord's sacrificial love.

In the light of these developments, some of the acts of the Antioch assembly assume an extraordinary significance: the decision to send, as an ecumenical gesture, two leaders of the community, Barnabas and Saul, to take help to Jerusalem for the poor; the decision, taken during the assembly, to send the same Barnabas and Saul on a universal mission so as not to keep for themselves apostles for whom the whole world clamoured; the desire of Ignatius to correspond with neighbouring assemblies and their bishops; the concern that these churches should send a representative to Antioch to take part in the assembled community's thanksgiving service. It is possible to say that in contrast with the particularism of the Jerusalem community, Antioch offers the example of the life of an assembly in which attention is focused on everything that can be a sign of universalism, an act of intercommunion, a manifestation of the Lord's universal assembly of mankind ever since the temple was fated to fall.

The actions of the Antioch Christians provide some lessons for our modern assemblies:

1. The relation of the Christian community to the bishop is not a relation to a 'great prelate' or a superior; it is fundamentally a union with the missionary whose principal function is to bear witness to the assembly and to summon men to it.

2. The president of the Christian assembly is not primarily the administrator or he who offers sacrifice, but he who brings the Word, the apostolic word of the *kerygma*, the teaching word of the catechesis. This means that the principal reason why a priest is qualified to preside over an assembly is because he is Word-bearing, because his activity is 'missionary'. It is true that medieval Christians did not stress this characteristic, preferring to emphasise the aspect of sacrifice. This led to serious pastoral *lacunae*: the separation of the liturgical from

the missionary role of the clergy, and the exclusion of non-believers from Christian communities.

3. The Christian assembly met on Sunday not only to satisfy the spiritual needs of its members but also to be a visible sign in the world of the assembling of all the categories which divide humanity: Jews and pagans were united in Antioch just as the workers and the middle class should be united in the Christian assembly. How can the world fully realise that it is called to such an assembly, if it cannot understand the sign of it? On this point it may be asked if certain of today's assemblies are not so immersed in the sociological and the human that it is practically impossible for there to be a sign of this universal meeting together.

4. Christian charity is not only the result of philanthropic sentiments, but much more it is the outward and visible sign of the assembly's concern for all men. It is a form of inviting everyone to the true and final assembly. Such a conception of the assembly could, perhaps, deepen awareness of the super-natural element in charitable works which far too easily become merely administrative or philanthropic acts.

THE CORINTHIAN ASSEMBLY

A study of the Corinthian community is of special interest because this community, wishing to put into practice the ideal achieved at Antioch, was confronted with a series of unusually important structural problems; and the solution of these problems determined for a long time the pastoral activity of the Sunday assembly. We can trace at Antioch the broad outlines of a true assembly 'theology', a sign of gathering together. We can see at Corinth the way a Sunday assembly was organised to bear witness and to respond to this meaning.

Just as the Christian community at Jerusalem, derived from Judaism, encountered many difficulties in establishing a typical Christian assembly beginning with elements inherited from Israel; so the Christian community of Corinth, derived from paganism, encountered many difficulties in establishing its assembly, since it allowed itself to be tempted by the organisation of the pagan meetings. These difficulties were all the greater because the pagans, unlike their fellows in Jerusalem, did not possess a sufficiently large number of biblical texts, nor an appropriate number of psalms. Consequently, some elements of these assemblies had to be left to improvisation and there was a danger that there would be some confusion with paganism and that too many human elements would be given full latitude. Paul reacted to these dangers by forming a Christian assembly that would be unlike both the pagan religious assemblies and the Jewish worshipping assemblies. He insisted on the originality of the new form and emphasised that it proceeded from a 'tradition' (1 Cor 11:16, 23).

A SIGN OF THE GREAT CHURCH

Men are the same everywhere, whether they be in Jerusalem or in Corinth. It is not surprising, therefore, that one of the first problems Paul encountered was that of the separation between rich and poor in the *agape* that accompanied the breaking of bread.

> For in eating, each one goes ahead with his own meal, and one is hungry and another is drunk. What! Do you not have houses to eat and drink in? Or do you despise the church of God and humiliate those who have nothing? (1 Cor 11:21–22).

Probably the number of the faithful made it impossible for all to sit around a common table, so it was necessary to have a number of separate tables just as in a modern restaurant. But this division resulted in groups being formed by those with interests in common. People confined their interest to the guests at the same table and very soon all the others were ignored.

To remedy this situation, Paul put forward two arguments. By their attitude the 'rich' offended the poor: this was an argument based on ordinary good manners backed by a reminder of necessary Christian charity. But the second argument is doctrinal: Christians who acted in this way were being contemptuous of the Church of God (*ekklesia tou theou*); and we are not unaware of the meaning Paul attaches to the expression 'Church of God':

To the church of God which is at Corinth, to those sanctified in Christ Jesus, called to be saints together with all those who in every place call on the name of our Lord Jesus Christ both their Lord and ours . . . (1 Cor 1:2).

The assembly of all men, begun by the Lord at his resurrection, is a meeting of all men called to be saints (in Greek the verb 'call' and the noun 'Church' have the same root). This 'Church of God' will be realised only by means of local assemblies (also called *ekklesia*), made up of those who 'in every place' call on the name of the Lord and those who are brought together in the unity of God's great assembly. This concomitance between local assemblies and 'the Church of God' was more clearly seen in the days of St Paul than at the present time because the word *ekklesia* denoted both the local assembly and the universal Church. Moreover, a certain juridical concept of the universal Church has obscured for us the relation between the two forms of the Church. St Paul considered that the universal assembly, the realisation of which being the true goal of Christians, could be essentially achieved in the local assembly of the 'last days' in which we live, a time which was both a sign and a mystery. It follows that to despise the unity of the local assembly is equivalent to despising the Church of God (1 Cor 11:22).

In addition to the word *ekklesia*, Paul also has recourse to the theme of the 'Body of Christ' to explain the concomitance of the local assembly and the universal Church.

Now you are the body of Christ and individually members of it (1 Cor 12:27).

Even if the reference in this passage is no more than allegorical, Paul can already see the mystery of the Church-Body of Christ based on the celebration of the local assembly which also is the Body of Christ. It is not enough to say that the local assembly acts as a kind of deputy for the universal Church, thus enabling the local assembly to pray and act 'in its name'. Nor is it enough to think of the local assembly as the symbol of the universal Church. These juridical or symbolic concepts are not sufficiently Pauline to show that the local assembly is the 'sacrament' (the visible and efficacious sign) of the universal Church. Moreover, is it not the eucharist, celebrated on the local level, which builds up the Body of Christ? Certainly the local assembly does not exhaust the mystery nor the whole reality of the universal Church. But the latter, in addition to the eucharistic celebrations, includes a series of 'services' intended to assist the local assemblies, to further their intercommunion and to ensure their unity in the same faith.

This explains why St Paul considers any disorder in the local assembly to be a serious blow to the mystery of the Church, because it calls in question its most important function. Indeed the universal Church will never put into action the programme, given it by the Lord, of gathering all nations together, unless it achieves union in the local level. The organisation and structure of the local assembly are not primarily questions of rules and regulations, of ceremonial and aesthetics; they are necessary because of doctrine and the work of assembling all peoples begun by the Lord of heaven and earth.

This means that all the problems connected with the assembly over which the pastor presides should be solved by him in the light of this doctrine; otherwise the human solutions that are adopted will sooner or later reduce the community to nothing but an administrative unit, and worship will become a simple religious gathering that any pagan religion whatsoever could organise. Paul wished to answer the problems raised by the Corinthian assembly with solutions that correspond to these principles, as for instance in the case of the incestuous man who was to be excommunicated (1 Cor 5), the duties of women in communities (1 Cor 11:2–16; 14:34–40), or the role of the world in the regulation of charisms (1 Cor 12–13). Two centuries later these solutions had become canonical regulations. This explains why the *Didascalia* of the apostles, when referring to the obligation of every Christian to take part in the Sunday assembly, argues like this:

> Let no one diminish the assembly by absenting himself, nor diminish by a single member the Body of Christ . . . Do not despise yourself by dispersing the Body of Christ. Otherwise what excuse will those have before God who do not come together on the Lord's Day to hear the Word of life and to receive nourishment that will last eternally? (Canon 13).

The Body of Christ is, of course, the whole Church. But it is built up at the level of the local assembly: to absent oneself from this assembly is, therefore, to withdraw a member from the Body of Christ.

DUTIES IN THE ASSEMBLY

The primitive Church had to face many difficulties when it began to organise liturgical assemblies in pagan surroundings. Biblical texts were lacking and members of the hierarchy were not trained to carry out the duties and all the functions that were necessary. Furthermore, the faithful in many cases had been members of some pagan sect and tended, despite their conversion, to introduce pagan rites and ceremonies into Christian worship. The Holy Spirit compensated for these deficiencies by inspiring certain 'prophets' whose role seems to have been the proclamation of the Word of God in the assemblies. To others were given charismatic gifts of miracles or healing which, at a time when the marvellous was highly esteemed, could have Christian apologetic value. Some Christians also possessed a somewhat mysterious charism: glossolalia which meant that others had to possess the gift of interpreting their unintelligible words.

This charism of glossolalia or 'gift of tongues' played an important part in Corinthian assemblies, prolonging into ecstasy prayer (1 Cor 14:14), hymns (1 Cor 14:15) or even thanksgiving (1 Cor 14:16). Sometimes those speaking in tongues caused considerable confusion in the assembly because they all spoke at once (1 Cor 14:27). This was not a new phenomenon; it had been known among the old Jewish prophets (Num 11:25–29; 1 Sam 10:5–6, 10–13; 19:20–24; 1 Kings 22:10). It seems that it was given to the apostles at Pentecost (Acts 2:7–11) and to many Christians at the time of their conversion (Acts 10:46; 11:15; 19:6). If Luke considers it to be a sign of the universal assembly (Acts 2:7–11), Paul sees it rather as a sign of dispersion and division. He admits that this phenomenon may come from the Holy Spirit but he places it last in the hierarchy of charisms.

Now you are the body of Christ and individually members of it. And

God has appointed in the assembly[1] first apostles, second prophets, third teachers . . . Do all work miracles? Do all possess gifts of healing? Do all speak with tongues? Do all interpret? (1 Cor 12:27–30).

Several times in his writings, Paul returns to this subject without mentioning the apostles (Eph 4:11). In spite of certain differences in the lists, he always gives first place to the charism of the Word (apostles, prophets, doctors), then come miracles and healing, followed by charisms for the administration of the community (presiding, assisting) which seem to allude to the duties of the elders in Jewish and Judaeo-Christian communities, and lastly the gift of tongues and their interpretation.

By placing the charisms of the Word in the first place, Paul is faithful to the purest Jewish tradition. Had not the Old Testament assemblies been structured on the Word? Does not the triple hierarchy: apostles of the gospel, prophets of the Word, and doctors of learning, correspond to the Jewish hierarchy of Law, Prophecy and Wisdom? But it is also as a disciple of the Lord that Paul established this hierarchy with the Word at the head of the list. He believed that to meet in assembly meant 'to build the temple of the Lord', this spiritual temple that now constitutes the assembly which has gathered. If he gives so important a place to the charism of the Word, it is because they 'edify' (and this word of St Paul really means the actual construction of the new spiritual temple),[2] in contrast to glossolalia, even when it may be considered as a true prayer addressed to God. In the fourteenth chapter of the first letter to the Corinthians, the theme of 'edification' keeps recurring.

. . . he who prophesies speaks to men for their upbuilding and encouragement and consolation. He who speaks in a tongue edifies himself, but he who prophesies edifies the church . . . He who prophesies is greater than he who speaks in tongues, unless some one interprets, so that the church may be edified (1 Cor 14:3–5).

[1] Contrary to the expression used in most versions, we have translated *ekklesia* by assembly. The context of 1 Cor 12, where the question is exclusively that of the problem of assemblies, requires this translation which does not prevent, as we have seen, that there is also concomitantly the mystery of the universal Church.

[2] On this theme, see Bonnard, *Jésus-Christ édifiant son Église*, Delachaux 1948, p. 48.

So with yourselves; since you are eager for manifestations of the Spirit, strive to excel in building up the Church (11 Cor 14:12).

. . . When you come together, each has a hymn, a lesson, a revelation, a tongue, or an interpretation. Let all things be done for edification (1 Cor 14:26).

The letter to the Ephesians returns to this idea that the assembly is built around the apostles and the prophets:

. . . you are . . . members of the household of God, built on the foundation of the apostles and prophets, Christ Jesus himself being the cornerstone, in whom the whole structure is joined together and grows into a holy temple in the Lord; in whom you also are built into it for a dwelling place of God in the Spirit (Eph 2:19–22).

The assembly replaces the Temple. It is no longer built with material elements but with faith in the word of the apostles and loving obedience to the word of the prophets. Yet, even though spiritual, this temple is not only a place of worship and of the divine presence; in the eyes of St Paul, it is basically a place where all nations may assemble.

If, therefore, the whole church assembles and all speak in tongues, and outsiders or unbelievers enter, will they not say that you are mad? But if all prophesy, and an unbeliever or outsider enters, he is convicted by all, he is called to account by all, the secrets of his heart are disclosed; and, so, falling on his face, he will worship God and declare that God is really among you (1 Cor 14:23–25).

The words attributed by Paul to pagans who were received in the Christian assembly are to be found in the writings of the prophets where they are proclaimed by the nations who assembled in the Jerusalem temple.

. . . The wealth of Egypt and the merchandise of Ethiopia, and the Sabeans, men of stature, shall come over to you, and be yours . . . They will make supplication to you, saying: 'God is with you only . . .' (Isa 45:14).

Many peoples and strong nations shall come to seek the Lord of hosts in Jerusalem, and to entreat the favour of the Lord . . . 'Let us go with you, for we have heard that God is with you' (Zech 8:22–23).

Paul's meaning is clear: the more the assembly becomes a spiritual temple centred on the Word, the more the nations are brought together. Now we can see why Paul's concern about the internal organisation of the assembly's liturgy is always missionary in nature. He places the charisms of the word of the evangelising apostle at the top of the list and he believes that an assembly constituted in this way can be a sign for non-Christians.[1]

If there is good reason to distinguish *kerygma* from catechesis, it is dangerous for pastoral work to separate them. In any case, we think we have shown that the problems of the internal organisation of liturgical assemblies, at Antioch as at Corinth, were always proposed and solved in the context of the assembling of all men; in fact, the liturgical assembly seems to have been a sign conditioned by the demands of the missionary movement itself. It is true that the purpose of pastoral liturgy is the celebration of the mystery. But is not the mystery *par excellence* precisely this universal assemblying towards which the missionary is working (Eph 3:1–6)? It follows that the apostle, the bearer of the Word to men and the one responsible for the assemblying of all men, is by right the head of the assembly's pastoral liturgy.

It certainly seems that, both in Corinth and in Antioch, the Christians were well aware that the Church fulfils its mission of assemblying only in the liturgical assembly. There is no mission apart from the eucharist; one contributes to the other. The Church cannot claim to be the people 'who are already redeemed' without proclaiming itself to be, and to wish to be, sent to those 'who are not yet redeemed'. It is truly an 'assembly' only at the moment when it understands itself as 'meant to assemble'.

AN ASSEMBLY THAT UNDERSTANDS

The Word at the heart of the assembly is meant to clarify the meaning of the assembly; not merely to give a human understanding which would go no further than the meaning of the words, but an understanding of faith which is the response to the *kerygma* of the gospel and an understanding of love which recognises God's

[1] This position is the contrary of that proposed by A.-M. Roguet, 'La pastorale liturgique' in *L'Église en prière*.

plan and lovingly co-operates with it. Paul seems extremely concerned about this understanding of the assembly. Between a word which can help the assembly and a word which can be pleasing only to God, he unhesitatingly prefers the former:

> For one who speaks in a tongue speaks not to men but to God . . . he who prophesies edifies the church . . . He who prophesies is greater than he who speaks in tongues . . . (1 Cor 14:2–5).

> For if I pray in a tongue, my spirit prays but my mind is unfruitful (1 Cor 14:14).

> . . . in church I would rather speak five words with my mind, in order to instruct others, than ten thousand words in a tongue (1 Cor 14:19).

Therefore, religious value alone is not enough to gain priority in the assembly, even though this value be of prayer and reference to God. Judgement should be based on relation to the 'edification' of an intelligent assembly. Therefore there are to be no 'tongues' without interpretation, no formulas or rites which become magic because incomprehensible, nor any elements which place souls only in a religious contact with God and do not provide for the instruction and edification of the community. This certainly defines the respective positions of private and collective prayer in the liturgical assembly.

Paul's meaning is clear. His argument follows a logical pattern. If the assembly is truly the spiritual temple, which is erected so that it may become the sign of the coming together of all men, and if sacrifice is offered only in the spirit of faith and obedience to the plan of God, everything in it should be understood.

> Otherwise, if you bless with the spirit, how can any one in the position of an outsider say the 'Amen' to your thanksgiving when he does not know what you are saying? For you may give thanks well enough, but the other man is not edified (1 Cor 14:16–17).

Paul is reminded of the confusion of tongues at the tower of Babel. Is an assembly, whose purpose is to unite all men in a common understanding, to give the appearance of a new Babel where men appear to behave barbarously to one another?

> . . . if you in a tongue utter speech that is not intelligible how will

any one know what is said? For you will be speaking into the air. There are doubtless many different languages in the world, and none is without meaning, but if I do not know the meaning of the language, I shall be a foreigner to the speaker . . . So with yourselves; since you are eager for the manifestations of the Spirit, strive to excel in building up the church (1 Cor 14:9–12).

St Paul also recalls the punishment inflicted on Israel the day it refused to listen to the word of the prophets. God sent them only men who spoke an incomprehensible language (Isa 28:11–12). In fact, why speak plainly to men who refuse to listen? So Paul tells Christians pleased to take part in assemblies where they understand nothing that they have placed themselves in the same situation:

In the law it is written, 'By men of strange tongues and by the lips of foreigners will I speak to this people, and even then they will not listen to me, says the Lord' (1 Cor 14:21).

It would be impossible to describe better the essential characteristic of the Christian assembly and its functioning. First of all, it is not an assembly of religious worship but rather a sign of God's plan, a plan that builds a temple reserved for a spiritual sacrifice to which all men are invited. This sacrifice can be celebrated only by a people which acquiesces, in spirit and in truth, in full knowledge and understanding, to the Word proclaimed on behalf of the Lord.

Do we really possess this 'understanding' when we come together for the eucharistic assembly? Have we faith enough to refuse all that is 'barbarous' and language that is incomprehensible in our assemblies? Are we sufficiently aware that a liturgy, even in a living tongue, will remain incomprehensible unless it is interpreted in a way that will enable it to rekindle our faith and increase our powers of spiritual sacrifice?

THE APOSTLE, THE LITURGICAL MINISTER
OF JESUS CHRIST

In an assembly that is a true spiritual temple (cf. 1 Cor 6:19; 2 Cor 6:16), which really offers a spiritual sacrifice because of the faith of those who hear the Word, the apostle, the bearer of this Word and the father of the faith, is obviously the officiant. St Paul describes him as the architect of the temple (1 Cor 3:10–17). A year later, in the second letter to the Corinthians, he envisages his own ministry to Corinth as a true liturgy, which is just as pleasing to God as were the old sacrifices:

> But thanks be to God, who in Christ always leads us in triumph, and through us spreads the fragrance of the knowledge of him everywhere. For we are the aroma of Christ to God among those who are being saved and among those who are perishing, to one a fragrance from death to death, to the other a fragrance from life to life. Who is sufficient for these things? For we are not, like so many, peddlers of God's word; but as men of sincerity, as commissioned by God, in the sight of God, we speak in Christ (2 Cor 2:14–17).

Paul therefore gives 'thanks' that, as a result of his apostolic work and its tribulations, the fragrance of spiritual sacrifice rises 'in every place'.[1] The Word that he proclaims in his apostolic ministry he speaks in God's presence, just as the priest in the temple presents himself 'before God' to offer his sacrifice.

In the letter to the Romans, the definitive formulation of his thought, he alludes to the spiritual sacrifice that Christians never cease to offer up to God, 'they are to yield their members to God as the priest presents the victim on the altar' (cf. Rom 6:13); he tells them to 'present your bodies as living sacrifice, holy and acceptable to God' (Rom 12:1). Now who, save the apostle and the bearers of the Word, can put Christians in these dispositions? Thus Paul sees in his apostolate:

> . . . the grace given me by God to be a minister of Christ Jesus to the Gentiles in the priestly service of the gospel of God, so that the offering of the Gentiles may be acceptable, sanctified by the Holy Spirit (Rom 15:16).

The terms of officiant, liturgical minister, offerer, are not to be understood as mere metaphors. In them Paul means to unite the content of the new spiritual sacrifice and the clearly defined

---

[1] Cf. Mal 1:11 who announced the spiritual sacrifice of all nations, a sacrifice of fragrant incense 'in every place'.

role of the bearer of the Word. The whole Christian life, therefore, becomes an act of worship and the one who is responsible
for this life is made the officiant of this new worship.[1]

Nevertheless, the liturgical assembly keeps its distinctive
position. It is the true basis of the Christian's worshipping life.
Moreover, to bring about the necessary conditions for spiritual
sacrifice, he who presides possesses a still more efficacious word
than any he has used in his apostolic ministry: the sacramental
word, of which the kerygmatic and catechetic word are the
prelude.

Today the right to preside at an assembly depends on the
power of orders. But St Paul's theology is too specific to allow
us to define orders independently of the ministry of the Word
in the sense in which the apostle understands it. If Christian
assemblies contain rites and sacrifices presented by ministers,
their full value comes from the Word that created them; it was
a missionary word and a word of faith before it was a sacramental
word:

> For Christ did not send me to baptize but to preach the gospel, and
> not with eloquent wisdom, lest the cross of Christ be emptied of
> power (1 Cor 1:17).

WOMEN IN THE ASSEMBLY

Throughout its history, the primitive Christian assembly was
concerned to show the world that social categories were transcended in the union of the assembly. St Paul reminds the Corinthians of this principle:

> For just as the body is one and has many members, and all the mem-
> bers of the body, though many, are one body,[2] so it is with Christ.
> For by one Spirit we were all baptized into one body — Jews or
> Greeks, slaves or free — and all were made to drink of one Spirit
> (1 Cor 12:12–13).

But if Jews or pagans, slaves or free, are in every way equal in

[1] Cf. A. M. Denis, *Fonction apostolique et liturgie en esprit*, Rev. Sc. et Th. 1958,
pp. 401–436; 617–656.
[2] It will be recalled that Paul used the image of the Body in connection with
the assembly (cf. *supra*, p. 108).

the assembly, does it also follow that men and women are also equal?[1]

The answer given in the letter to the Corinthians is difficult to understand.

In the first passage (1 Cor 11:2–16), Paul requires the men to uncover their heads in the assembly, while he insists that the women wear veils over their hair.

> Any man who prays or prophesies with his head covered dishonors his head, but any woman who prays or prophesies with her head un-veiled dishonors her head (1 Cor 11:4–5).

This regulation points to a certain equality between man and woman because both can pray (*proseuchē*, denoting liturgical, public prayer) and prophesy (in the sense of proclaiming a Word in the assembly). Furthermore, according to contemporary Jewish and Greek culture, it asserts that man and woman enjoy the same freedom in Christ. In fact, Paul considers it to be a sign of man's freedom that he can present himself with uncovered head and a sign of woman's freedom and honour to cover her hair with a veil. This regulation has meaning only in a specified culture but it does seem to assure the freedom of both man and woman. Nevertheless, to convince his readers, who were no doubt tempted to conform to other customs, Paul proposes a series of arguments of unequal value: a mystical argument, the head of every man is Christ, the head of every woman is man (1 Cor 11:3); a rabbinic argument, man was created first and the woman must veil herself because of the angels (1 Cor 11:7–12; finally a stoic argument, nature imposes this law on man and woman (1 Cor 11:13–15). Dissatisfied, no doubt, with his own reasoning which was rather local and complicated, Paul then recalled the custom observed in Christian assemblies:

> If anyone is disposed to be contentious, we recognize no other prac-tice, nor do the churches of God (1 Cor 11:16).

However little we may be impressed by Paul's embarrassed reasoning, this passage seems to insist on the equality of man

---

[1] Gal 3:28 in effect places men and women on the same plane as Jews and Greeks, slaves and free men.

and woman in the same liberty of Christ, an equality which, however, is to be expressed differently because of the difference of the sexes. In any case, it seems to allow or to tolerate that a woman, as well as a man, may pronounce a prayer or proclaim 'a prophecy' in the Christian assembly.

It seems that the first Christians were not surprised when prophetesses proclaimed the Word in the assembly. The Jews were familiar with this practice. Anne's position in the Temple was as a prophetess and she must certainly have fulfilled her ministry of the Word at certain assemblies (Lk 2:36–38). Philip, one of the seven, who moved to Caesarea, had four unmarried daughters who prophesied (Acts 21:9) and the church at Thyatira, at the close of the first century, also had a prophetess named Jezabel who taught (*didasko*) the brethren (Apoc 2:20–21); and if the author of the Apocalypse is opposed to her, it is not so much because she was teaching but rather because she was teaching pernicious doctrines. In addition to these 'prophetesses', primitive assemblies also knew of women whom we would gladly call deaconesses were it not for the fact that this term today has a more precise meaning than it did in the first century when '*diakonia*' denoted every form of ministry in the Church, including that of apostle.

It may be concluded that in 1 Cor 11:4 allusion is made to the ministry of women in the assembly and that this is tolerated provided due observance is made of traditional discipline.

But after this passage on the role of women in the ministry of the Word and in prayer, St Paul lays down other more rigorous regulations:

As in all the churches of the saints, the women should keep silence in the churches. For they are not permitted to speak (*lalein*, which usually means a solemn or official discourse), but should be subordinate, as even the law says. If there is anything they desire to know, let them ask their husbands at home. For it is shameful for a woman to speak in church (1 Cor 14:34–35).

Was it to soften this regulation that Jerome introduced the opening words ('As in all the churches of the saints') which belong to the preceding passage? No one knows. In any case, this regulation has often perplexed exegetes and raises the delicate problem of its relation to the role stated in 1 Cor 11:5.

Moreover, the manuscript tradition of this passage is far inferior to that of the rest of the letter to the Corinthians; however, it is not bad enough for us to question its authenticity, especially since Paul adopted the same position in 1 Tim 2:11.

He denies woman the right to speak in the assembly. His decision is not an isolated one but it is in agreement with that of all the assemblies of the saints, Greek as well as Jewish. Like the collection for Jerusalem, like the missions entrusted to the heads of the Antioch community, or the representatives of all the churches at Antioch – a request made by Ignatius – and like so many other signs of intercommunion, the discipline adopted about the participation of women in the assembly is also meant to be a sign of ecumenicity and each community that adopts this rule conforms to the universal dimension imposed on those who come together.

Perhaps the situation at Corinth was exceptional and required special rules as 1 Cor 11:5 suggests; local needs are secondary in relation to the requirement laid on each assembly that seeks to be part of the universal pattern; however real these local needs may be, they can never limit nor reduce the catholic significance of the assembly.

Discipline applying to women in the assembly may one day change in the church. No dogma of faith would stand in the way, provided the natural and psychological differences that nature has introduced between the sexes are respected. But such a change would be valid only if it were adopted 'by all the assemblies of the saints' and if it were a sign of catholicity.

CATHOLIC PRAYER

Jewish synagogal prayer closed with a long formula which in the first century was called 'the eighteen prayers'. It consisted of a prayer divided into 'supplications', 'petitions', and 'thanksgivings': praise to God for his salvation, prayer for the restoration of the people and a listing of different intentions, from the cure of the sick to the conversion of sinners. It must be acknow-

ledged that the religious inspiration of this prayer is fairly deep –
God is seen with all those qualities that long meditation on
Scripture reveals – but the horizon of the requests is both
particularist and limited, sometimes even nationalistic; petition
is made for the annihilation of such sects as the Christians.

In their prayers, Christians certainly preserved the principle
but not the text of this traditional Jewish prayer, and they soon
gave it a universal significance. Earlier St Paul had asked this
of Timothy:

> First of all, then, I urge that supplications, prayers, intercessions, and
> thanksgivings[1] be made for all men, for kings and all who are in high
> positions, that we may lead a quiet and peaceful life, godly and
> respectful in every way. This is good, and it is acceptable in the sight
> of God, our Saviour, who desires all men to be saved and to come to
> the knowledge of the truth . . . I desire then that in every place the
> men should pray, lifting holy hands without anger or quarrelling . . .
> (1 Tim 2:1–4, 8).

It is as if Paul were directly alluding to the old Jewish prayer
and wished simply to add new intentions, open to the whole
human world and able to be repeated 'in every place' like the
sacrifice foreseen by Malachi (Mal 1:11); notice the multiplication of the word 'all' in these short passages.

Now at the end of the first century, Clement of Rome communicated to the church of Corinth the text of a Christian
prayer that parallels the Jewish prayer.[2] It concerns God who
'raises the humble and abases the powerful', who 'takes and
gives life', who bestows upon men 'the knowledge of his name',
who 'cures the sick', and 'frees from sin'. The two texts pray for
peace, but while the Jewish prayer asked this for Israel, the
Catholic prayer made a wider appeal: 'Grant concord and
peace to us and to all the inhabitants of the world' (Clem 59).

Both prayers contain petitions for the heads of governments,
but while the horizon of the Jewish prayer envisages no more
than the political restoration of Israel, the Christian petition,

---

[1] This accumulation of terms denoted the 'eighteen prayers' in Judaism.
[2] Yet it is foolish, in the present state of our knowledge, to establish exact
statistics about what was borrowed because we do not possess a critical text
of the Jewish prayer in its first-century form.

in response to St Paul's wish, embraces all the governments of the period:

> O sovereign Master, it is you who have given to the princes and leaders of the earth, power and royalty; by your marvellous and ineffable power grant that, recognising the glory and the honor that you have bestowed upon them, we may remain subject so as not to contradict your will (Clem 59).

This type of prayer, transmitted by Clement of Rome to the assembly at Corinth, in later centuries became the great litany of intentions, the *prex catholica* that is characteristic of the first Christian assemblies. To the assembly at Antioch we owe the thanksgiving prayer for the gathering together. To the assembly at Corinth we are indebted for the intercessory prayer of universal intentions, a prayer that is in itself a gathering together of men because it embraces them with all their needs in order to bring them to the Kingdom. This prayer is also a sign of gathering together because no human need is excluded from the assembly.

The liturgical constitution of Vatican II has restored this prayer of intentions to our liturgical assemblies. We should find in it the climate of catholicity which marked its beginnings.

AN ASSEMBLY THAT EXCOMMUNICATES

Conscious of their mission of gathering together and eager to remove all the prohibitions that protected the Jewish assembly, the first Christians sometimes showed an unreflecting generosity, welcoming into their assemblies obdurate sinners. The parable of the banquet (Lk 14:15–24) seems to reflect this optimism which transformed the assembly into a gathering of people who were compelled to enter by force (Lk 14:23). This would mean that men would find themselves passively united, without even the necessary minimum of conversion to merit to be gathered together.

So we see primitive communities becoming progressively aware that God makes the assembly possible, but a God who respects the liberty of those whom he summons and who expects from them a real effort towards conversion. The apostolic mission is not reduced to recruitment. It is dialogue and a call to conversion, an encounter and initiation to the faith. The Christian assembly should recognise the sign of their convocation as being the real conversion of those who knock at the door and also as being their obligation to perfect this conversion.

The Antioch assembly had already realised this need. Adopting the old Jewish excommunication formula: 'Do not give pearls to dogs', the Antiochene author refused to allow the non-baptised to take part in the assembly meal. The gospel of Matthew which was probably composed at Antioch doubles the parable of the banquet with that of the wedding garment (Mt 22:11–14), so as to show that those who take part in the assembly do not automatically take part in the final assembly.

> Then the king said to the attendants, 'Bind him hand and foot, and cast him into the outer darkness; there men will weep and gnash their teeth.' For many are called but few are chosen (Mt 22:13–14).

Matthew develops this idea in the section which he devotes to the doctrine of the assembly. Even there, where he describes the three categories of those who are invited to the new assembly, the intendants, the virgins, and the laymen, it should be noted that membership of these categories is not enough for inclusion in the final assembly: the 'wicked servant' will be cast out and will share the weeping and gnashing of teeth of the one without a wedding garment.

> . . . and will punish him, and put him with the hypocrites; there men will weep and gnash their teeth (Mt 24:51).

The same idea recurs in the description of the punishment imposed on the Christian who buried his talent:

> . . . and cast the worthless servant into the outer darkness; there men will weep and gnash their teeth (Mt 25:30).

As for the foolish virgins, the door to the banquet will be closed to them (Mt 25:10).

This doctrine which postpones the condemnation of the wicked to the end of time, at the final assembly, was soon seen to be inadequate; Christian assemblies found that some of their

members had to be judged and condemned to safeguard the
faith and the eschatological role of the community. It is to
Matthew that we owe the statement of a new position. Where
Luke speaks of mutual pardon (Lk 17:3), Matthew describes
the conduct of the assembly itself in the presence of the hardened
sinner:

> If your brother sins against you, go and tell him his fault, between you
> and him alone. If he listens to you, you have gained your brother.
> But if he does not listen, take one or two others along with you, that
> every word may be confirmed by the evidence of two or three wit-
> nesses. If he refuses to listen even to them, tell it to the church; and
> if he refuses to listen even to the church, let him be to you as a
> Gentile and a tax collector. Truly, I say to you, whatever you bind
> on earth shall be bound in heaven, and whatever you loose on earth
> shall be loosed in heaven (Mt 18:15–18).

The assembly as such benefits from the power of judging a
recalcitrant sinner, a power also entrusted to the apostle (Mt
16:19). In other words, the assembly has the right to refuse to
recognise one of its own who has halted on the road to that conversion essential to participation in the final assembly. It
was not a question of re-establishing the barriers of exclusiveness raised by Judaism around the assembly but, on the contrary,
of being able to read in the conversion of a man, a sign of God's
work.

Corinth gives us the best known example of an excommunication pronounced within an assembly. An incestuous man was
living in the community and it did nothing about it. Paul took
action. This member was to be excommunicated before the
feast of the Passover and for this purpose an assembly had to
meet to condemn him:

> For though absent in body I am present in spirit, and as if present, I
> have already pronounced judgement in the name of the Lord Jesus
> on the man who has done such a thing. When you are assembled, and
> my spirit is present, with the power of our Lord Jesus, you are to
> deliver this man to Satan for the destruction of the flesh that his
> spirit may be saved in the day of the Lord Jesus.
> Cleanse out the old leaven that you may be a new lump . . . celebrate

the festival, not with the old leaven, the leaven of malice and evil, but with the unleavened bread of sincerity and truth (1 Cor 5:3–8).

Excommunication was not only a sanction imposed by authority (for example, in this instance Paul) but a reaction of the assembly itself. Paul desired that the assembly should agree with him in the punishment so that the judgement might be the expression of the conscience of the community – not the exercise of a simple superior power. Would not certain sanctions imposed today by the authorities in the Church gain in validity if they were the expression of a local assembly?

In any case this progressive discovery of the limitations and conditions of the assembly made by the first communities enables us to see from the beginning a pastoral method of the assembly which was at the same time a pastoral method of initiation. Men did not enter directly into the assembly. A catechumenate or a community of penitents would help them to live or live again in assembly; it would teach them, by means of the necessary initiation, the faith and the conversion that will enable them to become members of the assembly. Mission, therefore, means helping a man to live in assembly or to teach him, if he has lost the attraction, how to do so. If there is no assembly in the preparatory mission, there is also no assembly without a preceding catechumenate.

CONCLUSION

Here we can consider together several attitudes which were prevalent in the first Christian communities, so that in the next chapter we can better establish the principles of the modern pastoral method for our assemblies.

SUBSTITUTION OF THE BANQUET HALLS OF PRIVATE HOMES FOR THE TEMPLE IN JERUSALEM

It was soon very clear that, even if the Jerusalem Christians found it hard to accept, the Temple could not become the centre of the assembly which the Lord wanted because it was

too much involved in the practices of a purely national worship
and too protected by walls of exclusion and separatism.

Only time and a few painful experiences enabled the Christians
to see that the eucharistic assembly had in itself the value of
the Temple, not only because the sacramental species assured
the presence of the Lord but more especially because it was a
true spiritual sacrifice offered in mutual love and daily obedience.
The results of this awareness became the normal practice for
the assembly pastoral of this time: as soon as the assembly
understood that it was offering a spiritual sacrifice, available to
all men, it was able to make a synthesis between liturgy and
mission and to become in this way a sign of universalism. When
it offered this spiritual sacrifice, it discovered its sacerdotal
quality. This quality was no longer reserved for a single offerer
but was shared by all the members of the assembly if only they
are grafted, by baptism and the eucharist, on the unique priesthood of the Lord. This understanding led to a new concept of
the hierarchy: not a hierarchy of those who offered sacrifice,
but of 'servants' who by their Word prepared the community
to enter into the proper attitude for the celebration of the
sacrifice and to unite themselves to the sacrifice of the Lord.

To fulfil the conditions of spiritual sacrifice, the eucharistic
assembly had to be 'comprehensible'. It did not gather together
to offer merely ritual worship, nor to perform an act of magic,
nor to plunge into some mystery: it is the faith of each one,
strengthened by the different charisms of the Word, that unites
the assembly and gives value to its sacrifice.

SIGNIFICANCE AT THE LOCAL LEVEL OF THE
UNIVERSAL MISSION OF GATHERING TOGETHER

In using the word *ekklesia* to describe each local assembly – a
word always reserved in the Old Testament for a universal
assembly – the first Christians recognised that the mystery of the
general gathering was present at the local level. The Church is
catholic, but this catholicity is first perceived and more especially realised on the level of the 'multi-localised' eucharistic
assemblies; and the least pretentious of local eucharistic

assemblies will always have more catholic 'significance'[1] than any church 'service' on a universal scale. Consequently, the local community should live and manifest its universal mystery; so the first Christian assemblies wished, after the unhappy Jerusalem experience, that their head be a missionary whose duties would free the community from the geographical and sociological forces that always threaten to confine it. Furthermore, these missionary heads of the Christian assemblies were able to formulate the theology of their apostolate, looking on the latter as a true liturgical duty and one meant to place the assembly in a state of spiritual sacrifice. After the disappearance of the apostolic generation, the first concern of the bishops who succeeded them was to maintain the universalist character of their function. They were able to achieve this by living in collegiality with the other bishops and by increasing the number of exchanges of every kind between the communities in order to lift to the universal plane, and thereby to explain the significance of, their coming together.

I cannot end this conclusion without mentioning the doctrine of St John. He wrote his gospel about thirty years after the authors whose books we have just analysed, so that he had time to synthesise the thought of his predecessors and to draw some definitive conclusions.

But in spite of the interval that separated him from the events that we have just related, John continued to be deeply concerned about the polemics they had brought to light: his attitude to the Temple is at times as virulent as that of Stephen (Acts 7:46–50); in any event, his attitude is as clear as St Matthew's. But John saw better than the others how the person of the Lord himself had replaced the Temple:

Destroy this temple and in three days I will raise it up (Jn 2:19).[2]

[1] Sacramental significance. Cf. Atanasief, *Le sacrement de l'assemblée*, Intern. Kirch. Zeit. 1956, pp. 200–213, because the eucharistic assembly really 'effects' and signifies the Church, the Body of Christ.

[2] We have already pointed out how John juxtaposes the description of the wedding feast of Cana with that of the purification of the temple of Jerusalem (Jn 2:1–11 and 2:13–22) just as Matthew did in contrasting the temple of Jerusalem (Mt 21:12–17) and the nuptial banquet room (Mt 22:1–10).

But, especially in the fourth chapter of his gospel, St John reports the lively polemics that divided primitive Christian communities concerning the place of the assembly. Christ was in Samaria near Jacob's well, where the hellenistic Christians who had been driven from Jerusalem inaugurated the 'mission' outside the city (Acts 8:4–8). John recalls that this mission began without apostolic agreement because they were still too closely linked with the Judaeo-Christian structures of the holy city (Acts 8:14). If Samaria has become Christian, this was not due to Jerusalem, nor to the apostles. John knows this and is reminded of a prophecy made by Christ to his apostles on this subject:

> For here the saying holds true, 'One sows and another reaps.' I sent you to reap that for which you did not labour; others have laboured, and you have entered into their labour (Jn 4:37–38).

This passage shows quite clearly[1] that John's milieu was that of the Hellenistic Christians who had discovered the catholic significance of their assembly. Therefore we can understand why John chose to place in this episode in Samaria the most complete definition of the assembly that is found in the New Testament:

> Jesus said to her, 'Woman, believe me, the hour is coming when neither on this mountain nor in Jerusalem will you worship the Father. You worship what you do not know; we worship what we know for salvation is from the Jews. But the hour is coming, and now is, when the true worshippers will worship the Father in spirit and truth, for such the Father seeks to worship him' (Jn 4:21–23).

Thus the new assembly is one that offers worship 'in spirit', the spiritual sacrifice for which the primitive assemblies were erected. But in St John's eyes, this spirit is the Spirit who raised Christ from the dead and who made him the Lord of the glory of the universe, communicating himself in the sacraments and in the signs of this assembly. The spiritual sacrifice that the Christian assembly offers God is, therefore, that of the Spirit of the Risen Lord.

[1] This is the thesis of O. Cullmann, *L'opposition de Jérusalem, motif commun de la théologie johannique et du monde ambiant*, N.T.S. 1959, pp. 157–173.

The new assembly also offers worship 'in truth' in the sense that it truly accomplishes and totally fulfils the prophecies that announced the new liturgy at Jerusalem. The Christian who takes part in a gathering outside the temple should have no complex about the Jew who goes up to his temple; the prophecies certainly referred to him, and he is in the process of fulfilling God's plan.

The assembly of spiritual sacrifice, an assembly signifying the universal gathering together – these two, it seems, are the two most central points in the theology of the first Christian assemblies. For the sake of our twentieth-century assemblies there must now be formulated, in a final and more pastoral chapter, the conclusions established by the first Christians as the result of their own experience.

4

The laws of our Christian assemblies

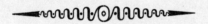

THE ASSEMBLY AND THE GATHERING
FOR WORSHIP

All religions have their gatherings whose purpose is to give God public worship through which man acknowledges his dependence on the forces that transcend and direct his life.[1] The Christian religion makes these values its own but transcends them by transforming a simple gathering for worship into an assembly, a sign of the coming together that the God of revelation effects in mankind. Its organisation does not rest merely on 'religion', it presupposes 'faith' in God's work and in the significance of this work.

This understanding of the assembly is essential if we are to appreciate the many elements which the liturgy contains. To quote one example among many: Christians who took part in the assembly soon began to be concerned about those who were absent, as if to include them in spirit. With this in mind, visits were paid to them and even today's ritual contains formulas for 'visits to the sick' which, with the reading of the Word, the singing of a psalm, a prayer, and communion, seem in some sort a reflection of the assembly celebrated on Sunday.

> O eternal and all powerful God, the final salvation of those who believe, hear the prayers we address to your goodness so that our sick brother may recover his health and give you thanks in our assembly.

[1] Too many catechetical works limit themselves to this one point of view. The assembly seems to them to be no more than a social manifestation of the virtue of religion. They have been able to rescue the liturgy from the individualism in which it was trapped but they are powerless to throw real light on the assembly.

O God, the sole support of human weakness, show your power in coming to the help of your sick servant, who, through the action of your love, may present himself safe and sound in the midst of your holy assembly (first and third prayers in the Mass for the sick).

Taking the doctrine of the assembly as the basis for a definition of the liturgy, it is possible to make a more adequate distinction between liturgical acts and what are called 'devout exercises'. A too juridical idea of them actually divides celebrations into two categories, depending on whether they appear or not in the liturgical books approved by Rome. This leads to real absurdity. A Sunday assembly held by a catechist or a deacon in an African or Latin American country is only a 'pious exercise' but the blessing of a belt in honour of St Joseph (which has the privilege of being included in the Roman Ritual appendix 11,1) merits the title of 'liturgical'! Yet it is obvious that a Sunday celebration without a priest, but presided over by the bearer of the Word and by the representatives of the bishop, is altogether more significant than some isolated blessing.

The assembly theme can also obviate paradoxes concerning the monastic office, especially when it is recited by religious women. This office is the direct prolongation of the Eucharist and the Eucharist is necessarily the local assembly. There is no reason to look for some kind of vicarious ecclesiastical delegation to justify a monastic assembly that carries its own justification and – with reservations to be noted later – accounts for the essential significance of the liturgical assembly.

Lastly, the idea of assembly can help to clarify the relations between private prayer and communal prayer. If Christian assemblies were no more than simple gatherings for worship, it would merely be necessary to respect the desire of each participant for private prayer and the gathering could become an occasion when people join together for private prayers. The objection of one who says: 'I cannot pray during Mass', is at once both true and false: true, because he must pray personally; false, because this prayer, in the assembly, cannot spring from himself. The Christian receives his prayer from the assembly; there he hears a Word which calls him, first to silent prayer, then to communal prayer; he takes part in the meditation of a gradual psalm which ends in prayer; he hears the words of the celebrant's thanksgiving and associates himself with it by means of different acclamations. In other words, he prolongs, explains, personalises the prayer lived in the assembly. How many changes would be necessary in the pastoral presentation of the Sunday Masses so that they would really gather together all the personal prayers in Christ's prayer to his Father.

PARTICIPATION IN THE ASSEMBLY

To describe and justify the act of spiritual sacrifice accomplished by the whole assembly, the term 'the priesthood of the faithful' is sometimes used, but it is ambiguous because it tends to separate the faithful from the ministers. In reality, the fundamental priesthood which is exercised in the assembly is that of the whole people, both the faithful and the ministers.

Now this priesthood of the holy people consists in making acts of love and obedience to God's plan in accordance with Christ's act of love and obedience, that is, the sacrifice of the cross. In fact, throughout his life and in the most lowly tasks the Christian (both the faithful and the priest) exercises this spiritual priesthood and gives worshipping value to his apostolic (Rom 15:15–16) and moral (Rom 12:1) commitment. In the heavenly assembly where there is 'no temple in the city' (Rev. 21:22), the priesthood of the eternal liturgy will be nothing else than the love of all the elect for each other and for God, lived in the love of the Father and the Lord. In the priesthood of the people, whose apprenticeship is continuously taking place, what is the role of the liturgical assembly?

In the first place, at the psychological level, it is a kind of 'intensified time' in which the Word of God, proclaimed and understood, places Christians at the level of this spiritual priesthood by calling them to obedience and love; it is an 'intensified time' in which, more explicitly than in daily life, there is experienced that ontological relationship uniting the Christian to the Lord, without which every offering of self would be vain.

But it is especially in its order as a 'sign' that the full meaning of the assembly may be seen. It is the privileged moment in which the Lord fulfils the coming together of mankind in his Kingdom, and in which all social categories are transcended. Each member of the assembly takes on himself this value of the assembly as a sign, expresses it by gestures and words and accepts the role of one who 'gathers together' in his daily life.

This doctrine of the assembly demands active participation. The faithful do not come to 'assist' at a priest's Mass; this would be a kind of 'clericalising' of the assembly, reducing it to one priest, forgetting his character of 'servant' or the priestly character of the united assembly. Nor do the faithful come 'to pray together' or 'to sing together' (and the reaction of those who protest against such infringements of their freedom is understandable). Participation in the true assembly supposes that the faithful are brought together first of all (and on each subsequent occasion) by the Word which is contained in the liturgy. Only at the close of this initiation, renewed on each occasion, should the faithful adopt a position, answer or sing. In this way, participation becomes a sign of the coming together of the elect in the Kingdom. It is an expression of the spiritual sacrifice that has marked the whole week or the whole day.

So many attempts at participation have come to nothing because the priests have begun by appealing to arguments of the natural, social or psychological order, without attempting to lift the congregation to the level of faith, by means of the homily, the commentary and the whole pastoral significance of the Word. That is, the assembly should be able to comprehend and perfectly understand the spiritual significance of all that is said and done in the eucharistic meeting, because all this is meant to 'build up' the assembly. The problem of the understanding of the assembly does not stop with the problem of language, even in the native tongue; the liturgy will remain incomprehensible if faith does not inform the culture of the faithful and does not help them to discover the interdependence between their daily life of bearing witness and their liturgical life in assembly.

DUTIES IN THE ASSEMBLY

'Functions' in the assembly are 'services' intended to make it aware of the spiritual sacrifice which it is offering. There can be no question, as in Jewish and pagan religions, of clerical duties created independently of the assembly. Every attempt to isolate the celebrant, to make his priesthood an absolute or his Mass a celebration to which the faithful only come to be present, reduces the Christian assembly to a gathering that is pagan or Jewish in form. In the same way the attempt to isolate the bishop and to transform him into an 'unctuous' and pontificating 'prelate' amounts to endowing him with characteristics that have no relation to his pastoral and missionary function.

It is because the priesthood of the priest is essentially a 'service' of the assembly, guaranteeing the validity of its own priesthood, that the priest cannot celebrate Mass unless at least one person is present. It is regrettable that bishops often celebrate Sunday Mass far from any assembly in the privacy of their own chapel.

Faithful to the spirit of the second epistle to the Corinthians, like St Paul, we must endeavour to define all functions in relation to the assembly and in the role that they play to make it more living and true.

THE BISHOP

The bishop is the effective presiding official of all assemblies, even of those that meet when he is not present. Our gatherings continue the experience of those at Antioch whose meetings depended on Paul and Barnabas, their heads (1 Cor 5:4) even when the apostles were away (Acts 13:1-3), or of those in Corinth who met together with Paul who was present in spirit. It might be asked if it would not be suitable to increase the number of bishops so that they might be closer to their local assemblies and be able to preside over them more frequently.[1] Of course, no bishop could ever preside over all the assemblies under his care, but these assemblies must be in communion with the bishop who is responsible for the mission, the primary

[1] As is known, political or administrative reasons have prevented an increase in the number of bishops in the West.

bearer of the Word and the sign of catholicity and universality. It is this which obliges the local assembly to lift itself to the universal level of the Church's mission.

But this communion of the assembly with the bishop should be manifest.

On the side of the bishop, every effort must be made to make him an effective sign of catholicity through his collegiality with the other bishops, through the care which he shares with his faithful for the universal mission of the Church and its dialogue with the world. The relations of the bishop with his priests and assemblies should be on another plane than that of discipline and administration so that he appears not just as a super-prefect or a superior, but as the chief bearer of the missionary word and the one primarily responsible for the assembly. When the bishop takes part in a local assembly, it would be regrettable if his prelatial or pontifical character should obscure the real reason of his presence: to give the assembly a universal significance and to make it a visible sign of the gathering together that the Church is meant to realise in the world. It is because the bishop is the first missionary of the diocese that he has the right to preside.

On the side of the assembly, some signs of the spiritual presence of the bishop should be stressed and one of these is the priest who presides over the assembly. At the essential and the ontological level, the priest is the bishop's representative because he shares in his charism of the *presbyterium*. An example which deserves our attention and which will enable us to understand the way the priest represents the bishop in the assembly is the power to absolve sins in the sacrament of penance. Not every priest can exercise this power and a priest of another diocese cannot do so automatically; he must belong to the *presbyterium* of the bishop. His power to absolve from sin is, in fact, a specific application of the bishop's more general power to call and to draw men, sinners included, into the assembly.[1]

The priest is also the bishop's witness in the assembly, through his desire to celebrate the liturgy according to his

---

[1] On this question, see *La pénitence est une célébration*, Biblica (*Paroisse et Liturgie* series, no. 58), 1963.

directives. This discipline reveals the bishop's presence. Although it is traditional for there to be this sign of uniformity, it is also traditional for the priest in his parish to enjoy a certain liberty. At Rome, for example, when the Gelasian Sacramentary was being prepared, priests could choose readings and prayers which were not necessarily those chosen by the pope. The unity of the *presbyterium* with the bishop is often poorly served by a too rigid uniformity which fails to take into account the special needs and the level of faith of each community. Moreover, would it not be one way in which the bishop could show the essentially missionary character of his function, if he were to make it possible for each assembly to live its own relation to the world?

The assembly possesses other signs of the bishop's presence: he exercises his role of leader in prayer by suggesting intentions for it. In the past he has done this by the *oratio imperata*; now he can do this by proposing intentions to be inserted into the common and *catholic* prayer which each assembly should offer to the Father. The bishop is the privileged bearer of the Word to the assemblies: there his letters are read first, they truly 'gather together' the faithful and open to them the universal significance of their assembly, unless, of course, they are limited to theology or direct the attention of the faithful to secondary points. In some recently built churches special provisions have been made for the bishop's 'throne' so that it may be a permanent symbol, even though rarely used, of the spiritual presence of the true president of the assembly.

THE CELEBRANT[1]

The Christian assembly has, as its first 'servant', a president. He is not one who offers sacrifice, in the Jewish and pagan sense, but a man whose duty it is to give the assembly its true sign of 'coming together' and to make it possible for it to celebrate the spiritual sacrifice in accordance with that of Christ. Three essential elements of this duty must be pointed out.

[1] See the study of Lecuyer, Le célébrant, La Maison-Dieu 61 (1960), pp. 5–29 and that of Mgr Himmer, Le célébrant, Rev. Dioc. Tournai 1960, pp. 466–476.

a) *The president directs the assembly.* As director of the assembly, the president selects the reading and the hymns, gives guidance for the homily and the commentary, names the ministers who perform subordinate duties. In eucharistic assemblies his role is partly limited by the rubrics but he can act more freely in other assemblies, such as the celebration of the Word and certain sacraments and sacramentals. The president is not so much the official of worship who applies pre-established rules but rather the one who organises the assembly, who builds it up according to the form of the Body of Christ, who transforms a nondescript crowd into a hierarchical and understanding people.

This direction of the assembly by the celebrant could have an important application in the present reform. If it is true, for example, that the celebrant is meant to transmit the Word of God integrally, and even the prayers handed down by tradition; it is also true that he knows the way this Word will be received by the members of the assembly. The Word of God is not only the sound that comes from the lips of the prophet but it also includes hearing and understanding. An assembly president who was not concerned about anything more than the faithful proclamation of texts would be doing only part of his work, he would not be creating 'an intelligent assembly' such as Paul wanted in Corinth.

Certainly the homily is the best means of fulfilling this mission but it seems that this can be perfectly successful only if the celebrant enjoys the privilege of adapting texts to his own community, at least for a time.[1]

b) *The celebrant, the witness of the coming together.* Just as the bishop is the head of the assembly inasmuch as he is the one *par excellence* who is responsible for the coming together in the Church of all mankind, so the priest celebrates Mass in a given community because, as a member of the *presbyterium*, he shares his bishop's missionary responsibility. The president's liturgical function begins whenever he calls men to the assembly,

[1] See Th. Maertens, *Le problème des oraisons en langue vivante. Paroisse et Liturgie*, 1964, no. 7; X. Dubreil and D. Hameline, *La réforme liturgique et l'évangélisation des pauvres. Masse ouvrières*, 1964, no. 208.

whether it be during a mission, the catechumenate or catechesis. That is to say, the celebrant is already 'an officiant' (Rom 15:16) when he shares the *presbyterium* of the bishop, often at the pastoral level, of the missionary task of the Church. Lest the assembly be given the impression that its president is no more than one who offers sacrifice or administers the sacraments, it is necessary that in the celebration itself, the celebrant be seen to be truly part of a whole missionary *presbyterium*, living in its fullness the relation of the Church to the world.[1] This dimension will be manifested in the way he expresses, in his prayer, the Church's missionary needs; in the way he strives to make his assembly a true sign of coming together in its own human context, and in the way he welcomes the faithful coming from elsewhere or Christians belonging to other classes or cultures.

c) *The president, the principal servant of the spiritual sacrifice.* The president knows that he comes to the assembly to offer a spiritual sacrifice and for this to be perfectly celebrated each member of the assembly must be recalled to the acts of love and obedience, the matter of the sacrifice, which must spring from and owes its efficacy to union with the memorial of Christ. It is the president's duty to meet this twofold requirement, first by exercising his power of Orders which introduces into the assembly the memorial of Christ's sacrifice, then through selected readings and commentaries awakening attitudes of love and obedience in the heart of the faithful.

As president, the priest is much more than merely the 'moralist' who reminds the faithful of their duties, or merely the 'teacher' who explains dogmas to them. He is the celebrant of the wonders effected both by his hands on the altar and in the heart of each person present. Because he is responsible for the assembly's spiritual sacrifice, the president will take care not to impose his own devotions or his personal ideas. He respects the family of the Lord of whom he is no more than a servant (Mt 24:45–51), and reserves special time for its prayer. Eager 'to celebrate well' with the greatest piety, he will also be 'president',

[1] On the traditional link between the celebrant's thanksgiving and the proclamation of the evangelical kerygma, see Audet, *Bénédiction juive et eucharistie chrétienne*, Rev. Bibl. 1958, pp. 388 ff.

learning how to preserve the greatest possible contact with the assembly, a really vital contact, instead of withdrawing from them to pray better alone.

For this reason we can be glad of the renewed obligation to have a homily. When the present offertory has disappeared, as is possible, then the celebrant's homily will lead directly to his thanksgiving: the catechetical word will become the sacramental word.

THE PRIESTLY TEAM

In many liturgical assemblies the celebrant is not alone: the priestly team of the parish or the religious community of a convent or a monastery accompany him, that is if they do not have to preside over other assemblies. Now the testimony of the clergy in eucharistic assemblies often seems like a counter-testimony: one member of the priestly team reads his breviary or hears confessions or even takes a rest in the presbytery. When religious communities invite the laity to their assemblies, even getting them to take part to some extent in their Mass, they are sometimes imposing a special rhythm or a different culture which separates more than it gathers together. How can Christians understand the meaning of the coming together that is at the heart of the assembly if they see priestly teams who care little about coming together themselves or about making a real assembly with their faithful?

It is fortunate that concelebration has now solved the problems that arise in this field.

THE DEACON

In the Roman liturgy the deacon was primarily the celebrant's servant, especially the bishop's. In the Eastern liturgy he was, in addition, the mediator between the celebrant and the assembly. In either case, particularly in Rome, he was responsible for the action of the community on the charitable and catechetical level, even on the missionary and apologetic level. In Rome the deacon served at the altar and looked after the giving of the community's alms to the poor. In the West he was charged with the catechesis and the missionary mandate.[1]

Thus, the one who was to exercise the diaconate at the liturgical level was the Christian most involved at the apostolic or charitable level. Here we find the clearest principle concerning the establishment of services within the liturgical community: the bishop is responsible for the missionary dialogue between the Church and the world; the priest-celebrant is asked to carry on this dialogue within the *presbyterium*, the deacon is the member of the community who is the most active in fulfilling the community's obligations to the poor or to those who need instruction. On every liturgical level it is an apostolic activity which justifies the choice of ministers: thus the eucharistic assembly is clearly the most intense moment of the mission of the Church.

This same principle should be respected in the choice of the liturgical groups chosen to form assemblies. Even though it is true that the faithful today spend most of their time in professional or family duties and find it hard to serve the community on two levels at the same time, it is still essential that the laymen who are responsible for the assembly should also be active in the apostolic life of the assembly.

It is possible that the diaconate will be restored to the Western Church. The celebrant could offer no more effective sign of 'coming together' than to call to his side at the altar those who in the community most effectively bear the burden of missionary and apostolic tasks. Would this not be the best way of showing that the liturgical assembly is truly at the heart of the relation of the Church to the world?

THE READERS

After the celebrant, the oldest servant of the assembly is clearly the reader. He is in some way the successor of the 'prophets' who proclaimed God's word in Antioch and Corinth. Under this title he takes part in the 'building up' of the assembly because he explains its meaning and in his spiritual priesthood renews a people obedient to God's plan.

[1] According to the Acts of the apostles, this was the function of Stephen and Philip. It should be noted, however, that neither was called deacon.

THE CANTORS AND THE MUSICIANS

Paul would accept only the charisms of the Word in the Christian assembly. This means that cantors and musicians have no reason to be present unless they contribute to an understanding of the Word and do not drown it by music that is too esoteric or too difficult to understand. The function of the cantor is best exercised in the recitatif of the meditation psalm that follows the reading. The cantor exercises practically the same role as a reader, singing the Word of God so that it enters more easily into the hearts and the prayers of those who are present. The work of the organist should be understood in a similar fashion as based on the Word: in fact, it might be said that an organist who perfectly fulfils his task by accompanying the singing adds solemnity to the Word and prepares hearts for the attitude of faith necessary for the spiritual sacrifice.

Cantors and musicians may be compared to those who spoke in tongues in Corinth when they turn their service into a so-called 'spiritual' concert which is altogether independent of the Word and therefore has no meaning in a Christian assembly.

THE DOOR-KEEPERS

Among the oldest of the minor orders, a special place should be given to the 'door-keepers' because their duty is highly representative of the meaning of the assembly. Standing at the doors of the church they are meant to welcome the members of the assembly, especially strangers; they act as 'baby-sitter' so that no member of the family need be absent and the whole household can worship together; they distribute Mass leaflets or remind those who enter of the liturgy in which they are about to take part.

This function of welcome is integral to the assembly and it is much more than a matter of keeping order. Through greeting extended to each and all, the door-keepers help them to understand the kind of 'coming together' that takes place in the assembly, they throw light on the 'sign' that the assembly gives to the world. By watching over the good order of the reunion, they contribute significantly to the 'edification' of the spiritual temple that the community constitutes and they collaborate in the growth of the Body of Christ where each one may find the place that is his and where he may add to the harmony of the whole.

It might be asked if the duties of door-keeper could not be performed by women. The art of welcoming is specifically feminine (we may recall the 'hostesses' in modern concerns) and might it not be a way of softening Paul's discipline about the intervention of women in the assembly?

THE COMMENTATOR

Western liturgy has introduced a new role: that of the commentator, a priest or a layman responsible for making clear the meaning of the assembly by inviting all to prayer and by initiating them to each new part of the celebration. Like the other charisms of the Word, the commentary is a service: it prolongs the celebrant's homily,[1] showing how the Lord's Word which is proclaimed in the readings and commented on in the homily, is accomplished in the sacrifice, in communion, in the dismissal to go forth in mission. The commentator is also one who 'brings together': he presents the central theme of the liturgy and follows its development during the Mass; and by showing the connection between the celebration of the Word and the eucharistic celebration, he situates the Eucharist in the life of the faithful.

CONCLUSION

However important all these duties, they are only a service of the assembly, they make it possible for the assembly to exercise its spiritual priesthood and to express in Christ the sacrifice it is entitled to celebrate. The liturgical tradition of the Church has always understood it in this way: in the eucharistic prayer the

---

[1] Th. Maertens, *Comment préparer un commentaire?* Notre Catéchèse, 1959, 96, pp. 1–10. So closely is the commentary related to the homily that it seems to be a function of the celebrant.

ministers refer to themselves as 'servants' while the assembly itself is sometimes called the family of God, sometimes the holy
people:

> We your servants and with us all your holy people . . . (Canon of the
> Mass).

If there is to be any reform in the duties of those who take part
in the assembly, this should be based on the idea of service and
entirely directed to the celebration of Christ's spiritual sacrifice
and that of his people and to the bringing together of Christians
through the intelligent and intelligible proclamation of the
Word.

THE SUNDAY ASSEMBLY

THE SUNDAY ASSEMBLY AND THE DAILY
ASSEMBLIES

Among the different liturgical assemblies summoned by the
Church, one alone is unique because of its solemnity, its meaning
and its obligatory nature: this is the Sunday assembly.

In reality the eucharistic celebration is carried out on two
levels: it can be understood as the expression of a need to
incarnate the mystery of salvation as far as possible within human
structures: so we have the Mass for a group of workers or for a
catechising class, a Mass in a flat or in an invalid's room, a
Mass for a funeral or a wedding. In all cases the meaning of
'coming together' is secondary and gives place to another and
more essential meaning: that of the incarnation of the mystery of
salvation in different social groups in order to meet man's
multiple needs. On the other hand, traditional meaning of the
Sunday assembly has always been the 'bringing together' of men
in the same transcendent act, whatever may be their needs or the
social group to which they belong. Many signs of the distinction
between the two types of eucharist may be found in the history
of the Church and its pastoral work. Thus it has never been
allowed to celebrate on Sunday to meet individual needs (marriage, burials). Moreover, for long it was forbidden to celebrate

the Eucharist on a weekday so as to preserve the Sunday 'meeting together' and when gradually weekday Masses were permitted their form was somewhat different even in the structure of the eucharistic prayer.[1] To remain faithful to this spirit, Masses on Sunday should not be offered for special groups and care should be taken not to give priority to weekday Masses, for example, those of the First Friday. This principle could lead to a new understanding of the 'parish Mass'. In many instances the 'parish' is no more than a sociological community especially when it corresponds to a village or to a homogeneous section of a city or to a group of 'parishioners' cut off from real life. Only too often the pastors of such a parish insist on the importance of the parish Mass without realising that they are going against the mobility of modern life and that they do not respect the true meaning of the assembly in such a situation. It is plain that parishioners who go to Mass in another parish often contribute to the creation of a more 'assembled' community than the one in their own village which may be too submerged in a social group. Therefore, instead of groaning ineffectually against the Sunday exodus of his flock, the pastor might do better to celebrate during the week a 'parish Mass' in the sociological sense of the word, so as truly to incarnate the eucharistic mystery within the village or the section of the city and to allow his parishioners to live the Sunday mystery within an assembly that may be more truly a 'coming together'.

Religious men, and more often religious women, frequently fail to take part in the Sunday assembly of all Christians. These religious frequently insist on their 'own' Mass, even on Sunday, even when they do not oblige the students in their schools to be present. Thus those who are marked more clearly than others with the sign of faith and the call to salvation exclude themselves from the Sunday assembly. What a great contribution these religious could bring to the Sunday assembly and what might be their influence if the laity could see them more often in their midst at this assembly. At a moment when religious men and women are examining themselves about their place in today's Church, it can

[1] There was no *memento* in the Sunday eucharist as late as the sixteenth century; the memento for the dead was not said on Sunday.

be wondered whether it would not be to their advantage to approach the problem on the basis of the place they should take in the Sunday assembly.

THE SUNDAY OBLIGATION

This leads to the problem of the Sunday obligation. It is curious that there is no mention in the old tradition of the Church of 'getting one's Mass', with all the individualism that this term evokes. On the contrary, it was the idea of assembly that was paramount in any statement about the obligation of Sunday Mass:

> Let him be faithful to come to the assembly so that no one, by absenting himself, will diminish the Church, nor lessen the Body of Christ by one member ... He who does not gather with me, scatters ... Do not despise yourselves by dispersing the Body of Christ. Otherwise what excuse will they have before God who have not come together on the Day of the Lord? (the *Didascatia of the Apostles*, canon 13, third century).

The obligation, therefore, does not consist so much in satisfying religious needs as in coming together and in building up in this way the Body of Christ.

According to the first Christian documents, the obligation bound the summoning bishop as well as his faithful. Of this St Ignatius of Antioch convinced his young friend, Polycarp of Smyrna:

> Make the assemblies more frequent. Summon to them the faithful individually and by name (Polycarp 4).

The council of Sardis in the fourth century obliged the bishop to hold an assembly on Sunday:

> that he allows no Sunday to pass without an Assembly (Canon 15).

These texts show the intention of the Church. They do not oblige the Christian 'to get his Mass', rather they invite him to realise with all his brothers the visible sign of the Body of Christ. They urge the bishop even more strongly to assemble his faithful, not only by calling them but also by giving the eucharistic meeting the true character of an assembly. How many Christians might be excused from their Sunday obligation so poor is the meaning or sign-value of their assembly and how equivocal is the call that claims to unite them!

THE ONE ASSEMBLY

For a long time the principle of the one gathering round the one bishop controlled the pastoral regulation of Sunday, and this explains certain measures taken by the first Christian emperors forbidding all public meetings during the time of the liturgical assembly. The principle was maintained somewhat unrealistically even in a city like Rome where the number of Christians reached tens of thousands. Nevertheless, facts had to be recognised and the Roman community was divided into several assemblies. But care was taken to safeguard eucharistic unity: the use of the *fermentum*, membership of the clergy in the same *presbyterium*; the division of the city into seven deaneries; the refusal to consider as a territorial jurisdiction the ministry of the clergy who were sent into the *tituli*; and still other measures. All of which reveal the constant concern of the Bishop of Rome to unite all assemblies into one. Also in Gaul, at least as long as the Church was bound by an urban structure, there was one assembly and priests who had been sent into the country during the week had to return to the city to join together with the bishop in one and the same assembly on Sunday. If the country people could not come into town every Sunday, the councils provided that the lord of the manor should at least represent in the episcopal assembly those who remained at home.

This principle of the unity of the assembly was still very important in the twelfth century because it was then the cause of conflicts between parish priests and members of the mendicant orders.

Today this is no longer the case: canonists have forgotten that the Sunday Mass was meant, above all, to signify 'the gathering together'. They have taken almost the opposite position and increased the number of Masses as far as possible in order to satisfy the needs of the individual. It is not purely and simply a question of returning to earlier practice. But at least it might be possible to modify canonical prescriptions by returning to a more correct theology of the assembly and by applying these facts in new cases as they arise.

In this way could be justified doctrinally the prayer meetings that are often held without priests on Sundays in Africa and Latin America. These assemblies have full liturgical value and are authentic signs of 'gathering together', not so much because they are an expression of real piety but above all because they are held in fellowship with the episcopal assembly. Likewise, it would be desirable that the liturgical assemblies that are held in the same district of a city be seen to better advantage as multiple moments of a single and unique assembly: that of the whole Christian community of the city, united round its bishop and the *presbyterium*, offering in several separate places, one and the same testimony of gathering around the Lord and assuming the obligation of the mission of the Church in the world to which this community never ceases to belong.

The principle of the one Mass might find fruitful application in religious communities. They have, in fact, for celebrant either a chaplain or a superior. More frequently than the pastor in a parish, the chaplain runs the risk of being no more than one who fulfils the religious needs of the community. But there as everywhere else, the celebrant is above all a member of the episcopal *presbyterium*, and under this title, one who gathers together. It may be wondered whether he might not give a better proof of his function by leading his community to the actual place of the Sunday assembly.[1]

CONCLUSION: LITURGICAL ASSEMBLY

The eucharistic assembly should be the sign of the gathering together and of the sending forth, but the parish in its present form cannot give this testimony. Too often exclusively 'Christian', it contains only 'the already saved' forgetting 'the not yet saved'; or it imposes on the latter, as a token of conversion, a way of life that has nothing to do with the faith. Some Catholic

[1] On this whole question of Sunday, see *La Pastorale du dimanche dans le monde moderne* (*Paroisse et Liturgie* series, no. 61), Ed. Biblica, 1964.

Action teams or priests are sent by the bishop to come to the aid of the spirituality of this parish. But the hidden or public opposition between the parish and the missionary teams constitutes a counter-testimony that can bear no fruit!

A parish too dependent on sociological factors, divided exclusively according to socio-religious investigations not deep enough to produce a community of faith, or too closely modelled on a little village, is so impregnated by the local mentality that it cannot bear witness to a missionary and universalist faith! In such a case the parochial institution tends to become absolute: the parish becomes so individualistic that it turns into a kind of 'preserve', controlling all administrative, catechetical and missionary tasks, requiring all the parishioners to be present at the local services. It is then exclusively at the service of an important function of the Church: that of the incarnation in a particular milieu. But it forgets or overlooks another equally essential function, the missionary testimony of the gathering of all mankind into the Kingdom.

Either way, the parochial assembly seems inadequate and unable to meet all the exigencies of a biblical theology of the assembly. The mystery of the assembly is not totally lived at the parochial level; it should be on the level of the collegiality of parishes in the episcopal assembly.

Of course, the parish priest can form a genuine eucharistic community: an assembly open to others, truly unifying all men and really bearing all the missionary intentions of the world, a gathering in which is expressed the missionary concern of all, and which 'sends back' into the world Christians eager to bear witness. It can indeed open communities in missionary regions, 'places' that the parish as such scarcely reaches. It can be vigilant lest it be lost in sociology, lest it attach too much importance to its 'territorial' jurisdiction, lest it lose sight of the truth that the movement of its members may oblige them to take part in assemblies other than its own.

But this marks the limit of the action of the pastor of an isolated parish, at least in the present situation. He may feel very close to the missionary teams, he may even have, in addition to his pastoral responsibilities, other missionary or catechetical duties at the diocesan level, yet according to canon law as it is at present, he is not responsible for these missionary teams. This responsibility belongs exclusively to the bishop.

In fact, only the bishop is at once responsible for the community of the baptised (a task in which the pastor fully shares), for the community of catechumens (the law gives him the right to admit an adult to baptism), and for missionary activities (for the Catholic Action chaplains and missionaries depend directly on the bishop). The bishop, who is at the same time celebrant, catechetical director and apostle, is therefore by his functions the only one who can really preside over the whole assembly. Only the Eucharist, over which he presides, builds up from within the assembly of men in the concentric unity of these three communities: that of the baptised, of the catechumens, and of the missions. Normally the parish assembly can make no such claim (or else it is ready to become a diocese), but it may signify this perfectly.

It will have this meaning in so far as it effectively brings together the laity that belong to these three communities: like the Eucharist, like the godparents of the catechumens and like the missionaries, it will have this meaning if it enables the laity who have received the Eucharist to be better godparents and better missionaries, but it cannot claim to direct the mission or to control the work of the godparents. In fact, in these areas the layman does not act so much as a parishioner but as one who has been given a mandate by the bishop.

This is the equivalent of saying that the parish assembly, as it is understood today, is but one moment of the episcopal assembly, the only one that truly meets the universal and missionary demands of the biblical assembly. It has been said that the pastor has the right to preside at his assembly only because he is part of a *presbyterium* which included the eucharistic, the missionary and the catechumenacal function. In other words, priests charged with missionary catechumenate functions cannot absent themselves from the episcopal assembly. The bishop is not the celebrant and, in addition to that, a missionary. He is a celebrant because he is a missionary. Therefore, it is necessary that priests responsible for the mission should signify their membership in the assembly presided over by the bishop, either by concelebrating with their bishop, or by working in parochial groups, and also by taking part in the eucharist celebrated at the local level.[1]

The pastor who presides at the parochial Mass does not do so because he is responsible for the spiritual needs of the faithful within a given territory. He presides because he is a witness and the sign of a *presbyterium* (but not the one responsible) in which the three signs of the assembly are united: mission, catechesis and celebration. On the other hand, when the bishop celebrates the eucharist and presides over the liturgical assembly, he does so not only as a witness and a sign of the assembly, but as one responsible for this action, as one who lives collegially with the bishops of the whole world. There is, then, no eucharistic assembly which can stand in isolation. The true meaning of its existence demands that, at every moment, it should transcend its own limits.

[1] For a case in point, see *La pastorale liturgique de l'aumonier d'institution d'enseignment*, P. et L. 1964, no. 3, pp. 286–303.